D1035704

NEW DIRECTIONS FOR INSTITUTIONAL RESEARCH

J. Fredericks Volkwein, *Pennsylvania State University*
EDITOR-IN-CHIEF

Larry H. Litten, *Dartmouth College*
ASSOCIATE EDITOR

How Technology Is Changing Institutional Research

Liz Sanders
Illinois Institue of Technology

EDITOR

Number 103, Fall 1999

JOSSEY-BASS PUBLISHERS
San Francisco

HARVARD UNIVERSITY
GRADUATE SCHOOL OF EDUCATION
MONROE C. GUTMAN LIBRARY

S.O.#
ado
1472

LB
2326.3
.H69
1999

How Technology Is Changing Institutional Research
Liz Sanders (ed.)
New Directions for Institutional Research, no. 103
Volume XXVI, Number 3
J. Fredericks Volkwein, Editor-in-Chief

Copyright © 1999 by Jossey-Bass Inc., Publishers, 350 Sansome Street, San Francisco, CA, 94104-1342.

All rights reserved. No part of this publication may be reproduced, stored in a retrieval system, or transmitted, in any form or by any means, electronic, mechanical, photocopying, recording, or otherwise, without the prior written permission of the publisher.

New Directions for Institutional Research is indexed in *College Student Personnel Abstracts, Contents Pages in Education,* and *Current Index to Journals in Education* (ERIC).

Microfilm copies of issues and chapters are available in 16mm and 35mm, as well as microfiche in 105mm, through University Microfilms Inc., 300 North Zeeb Road, Ann Arbor, Michigan 48106-1346.

ISSN 0271-0579   ISBN 0-7879-5240-0

NEW DIRECTIONS FOR INSTITUTIONAL RESEARCH is part of The Jossey-Bass Higher and Adult Education Series and is published quarterly by Jossey-Bass Inc., Publishers, 350 Sansome Street, San Francisco, California 94104-1342 (publication number USPS 098-830). Periodicals postage paid at San Francisco, California, and at additional mailing offices. POST-MASTER: Send address changes to New Directions for Institutional Research, Jossey-Bass Inc., Publishers, 350 Sansome Street, San Francisco, California 94104-1342.

SUBSCRIPTIONS cost $56.00 for individuals and $99.00 for institutions, agencies, and libraries.

EDITORIAL CORRESPONDENCE should be sent to J. Fredericks Volkwein, Center for the Study of Higher Education, Pennsylvania State University, 403 South Allen Street, Suite 104, University Park, PA 16801-5252.

Photograph of the library by Michael Graves at San Juan Capistrano by Chad Slattery © 1984. All rights reserved.

www.josseybass.com

Printed in the United States of America on acid-free recycled paper containing 100 percent recovered waste paper, of which at least 20 percent is postconsumer waste.

October 20, 1999

Contents

THE ASSOCIATION FOR INSTITUTIONAL RESEARCH was created in 1966 to benefit, assist, and advance research leading to improved understanding, planning, and operation of institutions of higher education. Publication policy is set by its Publications Committee.

PUBLICATIONS COMMITTEE

Richard A. Voorhees (Chair)	Colorado Community College and Occupational Education System
Craig Clagett	Prince Georges Community College
Eric L. Dey	University of Michigan
Jonathan Fife	George Washington University
Susan H. Frost	Emory University
Deborah Olsen	Indiana University

EX-OFFICIO MEMBERS OF THE PUBLICATIONS COMMITTEE

John C. Smart	Memphis State University, Department of Leadership
Richard Howard	Montana State University–Bozeman
J. Fredericks Volkwein	Pennsylvania State University
Mardy T. Eimers	University of Missouri
Dolores H. Vuca	California State University–Fullerton
Jacquelyn L. Frost	Purdue University

For information about the Association for Institutional Research, write to the following address:

AIR Executive Office
114 Stone Building
Florida State University
Tallahassee, FL 32306-4462

(850) 644-4470

air@mailer.fsu.edu
http://airweb.org

EDITOR'S NOTES

This volume of *New Directions for Institutional Research* provides insight into the way technology is changing institutional research. These changes run the gamut of our work and our profession, from determining the number of CD-ROM PCs and technical support skills needed for smooth office operations to assessing the impact of distance learning technologies on student learning and faculty workload issues.

The purpose of this issue is to look at how we have been affected by technology and to reflect on what we have learned and what we have left to master. The change brought about by technology has been both rapid and dramatic. Over the course of the past several years, advances in technology, broadly defined to include not only hardware and software but also networking, telecommunications, and other technology systems, have expanded our world and presented us with exciting opportunities, along with new and perplexing challenges. We have changed how we conduct our day-to-day operations as our static information gathering and reporting has been transformed by internal and external networks and interactive Web-based tools.

Thanks to advances in networking, the World Wide Web, and database software, we have greater access to current external information that allows us to provide a richer context for data interpretation. Because of this wider access, as well as pressures both to remain accountable to consumers and to meet legislative demands, we have often shifted from traditional internally focused studies to benchmarking studies with broader implications. Of course, the external world also has greater access to *our* information. Since we have little control over how these users interpret or use our information, we are often called in to reconstruct these interpretations and respond for our institutions.

The chapters of this volume show us how institutional researchers are addressing these challenges. Some authors provide road maps to the future; others share war stories and expertise from the field. The first chapter provides the reader with the groundwork needed for a discussion of technology trends in higher education. In this chapter, Susy S. Chan examines four critical trends in technology in the corporate sector: knowledge management, enterprise resource planning, data warehousing, and electronic commerce. She discusses the implications of these trends for higher education and IR. She provides the reader with a framework for understanding and preparing for our future challenges.

We then move inside academe to examine the changes that are taking place in the IR office. In Chapter Two, Joan Wells, Elizabeth Silk, and David Torres discuss the issue of expanding information access brought about in part by pressures for accountability and developments in information technologies.

The authors explore the changing role of the institutional research office from a data resource to an information and policy research resource and the new challenges that open access and third-party information users present.

In Chapter Three, Ed Schaefer and Tod Massa present an exciting look at how interactive the world of the institutional research office has become, with two case studies of the transformation of traditional data-oriented institutional research activities using current database and Web technologies.

Chapter Four takes a somewhat different approach to examining the impact of technology on the researcher. Trudy Bers uses the rapid explosion of distance learning, essentially a child of technology, to demonstrate the new complexities in conducting institutional research as a result of technology's impact on learning and pedagogy. She challenges us to rethink what we do and to look forward proactively in order to prepare ourselves for the future.

In the final chapter, I draw on all these chapters to summarize our experiences and what we have learned. I discuss the major themes that emerge from this volume related to information technology as a catalyst for change, information access and pressures for accountability, and the new information professional. I ask the reader to imagine how technology will transform our lives and what the IR office will look like in the not-so-distant future. With a new century just around the corner, surely a more distant benchmark is now needed.

Even in the short time between the preparation of this volume and its delivery to the reader, much will have changed in regard to information technology in higher education—new opportunities will have been realized, and new challenges will have presented themselves. The changes are rapid and relentless and will undoubtedly transform not only institutional research but also the face of higher education. I consider this an exciting time in institutional research and try to meet these challenges by looking for new ways to embrace technology in my IR office. Although many of these experiences have been positive, they have also provided new frustrations and challenges echoed by the volume authors. I would like to thank the many talented Illinois Institute of Technology students who have worked in my office over the past four years to make these technology solutions possible.

Finally, I would like to thank Susan Sheffey, director of research, Jewish Vocational Service; and Megan Fellman, senior editor, Office of Public Relations, Illinois Institute of Technology, for their insight and guidance in preparing this volume.

Liz Sanders
Editor

LIZ SANDERS is founder and director of the Office of Information and Institutional Research at Illinois Institute of Technology (IIT), Chicago. She also served as assistant director for IIT's National Commission and associate director of institutional planning and research at DePaul University, Chicago.

1

This chapter discusses four important trends in corporate information technology—knowledge management, enterprise resource planning, data warehousing, and electronic commerce—and their transforming effects on the academic workplace.

The Impact of Technology on Users and the Workplace

Susy S. Chan

Information technology catalyzes the transformation of the academic workplace and its people in many ways. Multicampus, high-speed networks, the Internet, and World Wide Web technology accelerate the speed and magnitude of this change. Across the nation, universities and colleges are assessing and defining how information technology can and may redefine teaching, learning, and scholarly collaboration, as well as basic administrative processes.

Technology advancement in four areas propels the pace of change: (1) new technology allows the digitization of information in the forms of text, images, sound, or large data streams; (2) high-speed communication technology provides the bandwidth for transmitting digitized data in various forms; (3) storage technology makes information access and storage efficient; and (4) rapid growth in microprocessors improves the performance of information processing (Oblinger and Verville, 1999). Internet technology allows different parts of the institution to collaborate by sharing information and provides students and other users with a new way to build relationships with the institution.

Internet-based network infrastructure is essential to this transformation and has several unique patterns:

- Virtual offices and teams, electronic collaboration, electronic messaging, and end-user information technology are turning organizations into "anytime, anywhere" workplaces.
- Decision support systems (DSS), executive information systems (EIS), and Internet technologies enable users and workgroups to access data,

resources, and their collaborators, serving as an effective means of sharing organizational knowledge.

- Networks and electronic messaging reshape an organization's internal structures and create new partnerships with external constituencies.
- Technology enables mass customization that emphasizes speedy delivery of services and products, based on individual needs.

Essentially, everyone in the academy—student, faculty, and administrator—will also become an information provider and consumer. Global, regional, and institutional connectivity necessitates new ways of doing business in higher education. For IR offices, this means new ways of analyzing, managing, and disseminating information, whether it is for decision support, planning, or assessing institutional effectiveness.

This chapter examines the impact on higher education of four information technology–based approaches that are gaining increasing attention in the industry as well as in higher education: knowledge management, enterprise resource planning, data warehousing, and electronic commerce. Although they are being used in the corporate sector for improving competitiveness and performance, they hold promise of a different type for the academy. Successful adoption of these approaches, however, accentuates the importance of information. They may redefine the relationship between users of information and IR. Within this context, this chapter examines each of these four transforming technology trends in terms of its nature of the technology trend in the corporate context, its relevance to higher education, and its implications for IR.

Knowledge Management

Knowledge can be defined as a combination of information, contexts, and experience. It merges information—the interpretation of data and facts—with intuition, values, and beliefs. Recent attention to knowledge management in the corporate sector arose from the recognition that the cumulative knowledge in employees' minds is critical to a company's competitiveness in the global market. Using network and groupware technologies, companies began to focus on structured ways of sharing knowledge across the enterprise. Collaborative technology, such as Lotus Notes, enables the accumulation, organization, and sharing of knowledge across the enterprise networks. A corporation can create a corporate memory and preserve its intellectual capital.

Consulting firms like Andersen Consulting and Ernst & Young are pioneers in knowledge management. Worldwide, these consultants contribute reports, methodologies, successful strategies, and solutions for particular problems to the knowledge networks. In addition, knowledge managers, typically with training in library science, are responsible for publishing technology and business trends on these knowledge networks. At the onset of each client engagement, a knowledge coordinator is assigned to pull relevant background information from the knowledge network. This coordinator also defines the format and process for knowledge contribution. At the project's conclusion, the knowledge coordinator ensures that all reports are properly organized and categorized for the repositories.

In essence, consulting is a knowledge business. These firms have huge repositories of knowledge. There are strong economic and strategic incentives for capturing what they know and organizing such knowledge for efficient access. Other types of businesses have also adopted knowledge management successfully. For example, Sun Microsystems built a distributed learning architecture to make training and knowledge sharing more efficient on a global basis. This helped the company become more responsive to customer support needs.

Knowledge management systems involve three basic types of knowledge repositories:

- External knowledge, such as competitive intelligence with analyst reports, trade journal articles, and external market research.
- Structured internal knowledge, such as research reports, product-oriented materials, and marketing materials and methods.
- Informal internal knowledge, such as discussion databases; the focus is on the tacit knowledge that resides within the minds of the people in the organization but is not in a structured, document-based form.

The development of a knowledge management system follows these sets of activities:

- Capturing knowledge through the creation or acquisition of documents
- Adding value to the captured knowledge through editing, packaging, and pruning
- Developing approaches to categorizing the knowledge
- Developing information technology (IT) infrastructures (such as wide area networks) and common desktop tools, such as Lotus Notes and Web, for the distribution of knowledge
- Educating employees on the creation, sharing, and use of knowledge

Several conditions must exist to support knowledge management. A mature and robust technology infrastructure should be in place first. Some level of knowledge structure, such as categories of services, products, and R&D disciplines, as well as multiple channels for knowledge transfer, such as remote access, teleconferencing, e-mail, and Internet, should be well acknowledged and practiced. More important, this approach views the organization as a human community capable of providing diverse meanings to information outputs generated by the technological systems instead of the traditional emphasis on command and control.

As pointed out by Davenport and Prusak (1998), successful implementation of knowledge management systems depends more on process and cultural change than on the technology alone. A strong process orientation is a prerequisite, and the development of a knowledge-oriented culture is critical for supporting knowledge sharing and creation. Andersen Consulting and Ernst & Young use knowledge management as a vehicle for transformation and strategic planning to reduce costs, increase revenues, and expand market share. Tying the creation of knowledge to employees' performance appraisal and incentives has been critical to this approach.

Relevance to Higher Education. Although less motivated by economic benefits, colleges and universities may find this approach useful because of several favorable preconditions. First, higher education, by nature, is a knowledge industry. Well-established knowledge structures and discipline-based processes for knowledge creation and distribution already exist. Second, knowledge management requires a strong cadre of librarians and information analysts to organize and manage information. Most academic institutions already have a staff of librarians. Some institutions could also draw resources from their library science degree programs. Third, the Internet has already been widely adopted by the academic community. It is the ideal platform for knowledge management. The Internet2 initiative, through partnership with government, higher education, and industry, is going to provide a leading-edge research and education network capability. This effort will demonstrate new applications that can dramatically enhance higher education's capability of collaborating in the form of virtual community and knowledge sharing.

Although these preconditions for knowledge management typically exist in higher education, others are lacking. First, the academy respects long-established academic disciplines that transcend institutional boundaries. Therefore, the concept of intellectual capital has a very different meaning in higher education. Scholarly pursuit and curriculum are structured around academic disciplines. These knowledge-generating activities often reflect a faculty perspective. Transforming such a culture to an interdisciplinary and student-centered one will be a long process. Second, although the Internet provides a ready infrastructure for knowledge sharing, most universities and colleges have taken a grassroots approach to the creation of Web sites on their intranets. The information is rich but uneven in quality, consistency, and relevance. Without an institutional effort for mapping and managing knowledge creation, the availability of Internet and World Wide Web technology alone will not provide useful solutions. Third, unlike corporations, few universities and colleges can tie knowledge creation to performance appraisal. At best, they use an informal approach to encourage sharing of valued experience and insights.

Given successful solutions in these problem areas, higher education may adopt knowledge management in several ways.

Exchange of pedagogy. A formal knowledge network could be created to encourage sharing of pedagogy and instructional materials across institutions or within academic units. The Teaching, Learning, and Technology Roundtable (TLTR) initiative of the American Association of Higher Education (AAHE) was created in this spirit.

Learning of new technologies. A structured knowledge network for learning new technologies can support on-demand and self-directed learning. Many institutions have a hodgepodge of training materials on the Web. Organizing it into a knowledge network with a mix of knowledge repositories will greatly increase the pace at which campuses adopt technology.

Support services for students. A knowledge network for student-related services, from admissions to retention, could generate institutionwide interests. Current intranets need to be restructured to take a more comprehensive view of mapping information and knowledge pertaining to students. Some redesign of work process and knowledge sharing will be required.

Department of Education (DOE) Knowledge Network. At the federal level, DOE may take a leadership role in creating a knowledge network to organize and encourage the sharing of local knowledge.

Implications for IR. IR offices can contribute to knowledge management by providing reports and analyses to the internal and external repositories. Their insight about institutional issues makes them good partners of librarians in mapping information and creating knowledge structure. This role is complementary to what Wells, Silk, and Torres describe in Chapter Two as information architect, an emerging role for IR. Multiple channels of knowledge transfer and sharing, however, require different forms of presentation and organization of information to suit technology media. Knowledge itself may become a new form of data for analysis. IR offices also become active users of the knowledge base to disseminate information and to assess institutional responses to critical issues. If they are not involved as contributors or designers of knowledge management systems, however, IR offices will risk the opportunity to develop a knowledge architecture that integrates data from multiple sources and perspectives.

Enterprise Resource Planning

Enterprise resource planning (ERP) software is designed to model and automate the core business processes of an enterprise, from financial and human resources to logistical management. ERP's goal is to integrate information across the enterprise and eliminate complex, expensive links between computer systems that do not communicate with each other. This type of prepackaged solution has gained wide acceptance in the corporate sector as an alternative to building new in-house information systems. ERP decisions are often made on the promise of seamless integration and a process orientation. Fortune 500 firms were the first ones to adopt ERP solutions, particularly those with global operations like Owens Corning. ERP pack-ages provide capabilities for multiple currencies, languages, and integrated databases to support geographically dispersed operations. Prior to adopting ERP solutions, these companies also built extensive technology infrastruc-tures to support distributed data access and exchange.

After penetrating the Fortune 500 market, now ERP vendors like Ora-cle, SAP, and PeopleSoft are concentrating their efforts on mid-tier small companies, governments, and the higher education sector. The impending year 2000 (Y2K) crisis in information systems prompted a second wave of organizations to seek ERP packages as solutions for legacy systems. The promise of seamless business integration and migration from a mainframe to a client-server technology platform motivated these companies to invest heavily in ERP implementation. However, these organizations typically lagged in technology vision or infrastructure buildup. They had little expe-rience in technology-driven process change or organization transformation. Woeful tales are emerging about the implementation of major ERP pack-ages. The cost of ERP implementation could be four or five times the soft-ware costs. About half of ERP implementations failed to achieve the desired results because managers significantly underestimate the efforts involved in change management. There is a credibility gap between what ERP vendors promise and what a company can achieve even for a successful implemen-tation. Major corporations like Boeing and Kellogg are still seeking pro-ductivity increases, inventory reductions, and promised efficiencies several years after ERP implementation.

A traditional mainframe legacy environment, such as SCT's SIS or Ban-ner products, consists of separate systems and multiple databases for finan-cial, human resource, and other operational functions. Data integration is difficult, and information access is limited. Multiple systems mirror the organization structure of functional silos. Different divisions often define a data entity, such as "customer," differently.

In contrast, ERP packages are built on the advanced client-server archi-tecture and network infrastructure. These integrated systems promote both centralized and distributed computing. Centralization is enforced through an enterprise database and infrastructure standard. A data entity is defined consistently throughout the system, and multiple modules interact with the same database. Distributed user access and customization are provided through the client-server architecture. This moves data manipulation and report generation to user departments to allow dynamic data updates and query. ERP packages share these common features:

- On-line systems with few traditional batch interfaces
- One integrated, relational database for all data
- Clear definitions of all data items, documented in a data dictionary
- Efficient support of back-office transaction processing

- Templates for processes performed by best practices in a given industry sector
- Client-server computing, network infrastructure, relational databases, and graphical user interfaces (GUIs)

As the name implies, implementation of an ERP solution mandates an enterprisewide planning effort to redefine and redistribute resources—technology, data, people, and workflow. An enterprise system, by its very nature, imposes its own logic on an organization and on its strategy and structure. Data integration requires organizational consensus on data definition and access. Real-time data access and dynamic data updates assume that users have sophisticated knowledge about interrelationships among business processes. Templates of best practices map how workflow should be reengineered. Although some amount of customization is feasible, deviation from the process templates inflates the implementation cost and makes maintenance and system upgrading impossible. The high volume of data traffic demands robust network infrastructure. The underlying technology support is often absent because many organizations have not yet developed a capacity to support or use new client-server technology. Regarding organization structure, ERP software helps flatten the organization hierarchy by streamlining business processes and providing easy data access. But it also imposes a high degree of centralization through standardization of process, data definition, and data architecture.

Owing to this complexity, companies have to hire consultants to ensure successful ERP implementation. Implementation services could cost three or four times more than the software costs. As mentioned earlier, many organizations that undertook ERP projects had little experience in reengineering and technology infrastructure. The risks of failure are enormous. Even for successful cases, return on investments will not be realized within the first few years because the cost of transformation is so high.

Companies that had successful experiences stressed the enterprise, not the systems. They focused on the strategic transformation of the organization (Davenport, 1998). Owens Corning, a widely publicized case, implemented SAP R/3 (release 3) to replace 211 legacy systems. Prior to the ERP implementation, the company had fragmented systems and organization. It was also losing market share. The ERP solution enabled Owens Corning to integrate order management, financial reporting, and supply chain management across the world with the strategic goal to reposition the company in new markets. This synergy allows the company to work as a complete entity and manage its dollars, materials, people, and information for timely assessment of market position. Such an undertaking means a thorough transformation of process, people, technology, and organizational structure. In contrast, companies implementing only modules of ERP systems commit to less reengineering but report less significant gains.

Relevance to Higher Education. Although for-profit organizations are motivated by financial incentives in adopting ERP systems, many of the forces involved in enterprise reengineering process and technology requirements are applicable to higher education institutions. The question is to what extent higher education is able to find a management paradigm compatible with ERP's underlying requirements.

In the areas of financials, human resources, procurement, budgeting, and purchasing, ERP packages could be implemented by using a project approach, because the management model for these administrative functions resembles that of for-profit organizations. Streamlining redundant processes, fragmented systems, and conflicting data sources can reduce administrative costs and improve efficiency. Furthermore, an integrated system with real-time data access by college and department managers is a welcomed change. This helps distribute decision processes to academic units.

However, major ERP packages were designed to serve the corporate markets in different industries. Although for public sector clients, ERP vendors modify the software packages to suit the needs of government and higher education, the templates for best practices in human resources and financials may lean toward the for-profit models. Use of these packages also requires additional features, such as budget encumbrance, in the public sector. In addition, integrated student systems were developed specifically to meet university needs but may rely only on a small sample of "best practices." Institutions, which often seek "vanilla" implementation without customization, need to be aware of the commitment required for extensive process reengineering to fit into these templates. Institutions interested only in implementing component modules—for example, a procurement process instead of the entire financial process—need to recognize that some ERP packages are highly integrated. It will take additional work to implement only components.

For processes that involve major changes in academic process and faculty involvement, such as integrated student information systems, ERP implementation must take an enterprise approach to address necessary changes of academic policies and faculty behaviors. For example, an enterprise student system will support on-line advising that extends beyond coursework. Policies on registration, financial aid, academic progress, and degree audits all have to be clearly defined. ERP systems allow faculty timely access to data from multiple sources to advise students in a holistic manner. However, faculty members are usually least informed about student data and policies. In addition, it is difficult to enforce faculty compliance of procedures and policies outside of the arena of teaching. Institutions should not underestimate the importance of training users—faculty in particular—in the use of data, tools, and processes before ERP implementation.

Several universities reported recent initiatives in ERP implementation in the administrative area:

- Central Michigan University adopted SAP financial and human resource software systems with concurrent academic reorganization and budget restructuring to enhance reporting for cost and distributed budget decision support (Nelson and Scoby, 1998).
- Duke University adopted SAP for procurement processes and conducted a thorough redesign of the procurement organization and business process redesign (BPR) as part of ERP implementation (Foster and Herndon, 1997).
- Cleveland State University undertook a "vanilla" implementation of PeopleSoft's Administrative System and used BPR to facilitate the software implementation (Gage, 1998).

Aside from technical challenges, these universities reported similar experiences from which the following insights can be gleaned:

- Sufficient time must be provided to allow an organization to learn the new software. Tight timelines are necessary to contain costs, but the complexity in process change, new technology, and multiple systems requires time to work out processes and data.
- The need for user training is grossly underestimated. The complexity of ERP applications and distributed computing systems can easily overwhelm an "average" user.
- Culture and business process change that must occur in the organization often meets resistance if there is insufficient time to gain significant acceptance. Nearly every workflow will be new, and many people's jobs will be redesigned. Accelerated implementation could result in staff turnover and user reluctance.

Implications for IR. ERP implementation has strong technology and BPR thrusts. To ensure success, institutions are advised to hire consultants to drive the implementation process. IR offices can participate in three ways: as a member of the data architecture group to facilitate data definition and data access polices, as an internal trainer for database users, and as a designer of data warehouses, as discussed in the next section, to capture data from the moving targets in ERP.

The real challenge for IR offices comes after the consultants leave, when the system is in full production. The integrated nature of the database means that one change in a student academic performance record could immediately permeate to her financial and enrollment profile. This dynamic nature of data updates makes it difficult for IR offices to do time-sensitive data comparisons. In this sense, ERP systems are not designed to provide new functionality for IR purposes but rather to ensure internal data consistency, standardization, and user access. User ability to access data in real time makes users more self-reliant for operational and transactional data.

Yet the amount of available information may necessitate a different level of decision support or EIS support, which has not been the strong suit of most ERP packages. (For a more complete discussion of the support necessary from the IR office, see Chapter Two.)

Data Warehousing

Data warehousing is the process of collecting data to be stored in a managed database in which the data are subject-oriented and integrated, time-variant, and nonvolatile for the support of management's decision making. "Subject-oriented" means that a data warehouse focuses on the high-level entities of the business, such as employees, courses, and accounts. This is in contrast to transactional systems, which deal with processes such as student registration or payment of invoices. "Integrated" means that the data are stored in consistent formats, with consistent naming conventions, domain constraints, physical attributes, and measurements. For example, an organization may have four or five unique coding schemes for ethnicity. In a data warehouse, there is only one coding scheme. "Time-variant" means that data are associated with a point in time, such as a semester, fiscal year, or pay period. Finally, "nonvolatile" means that the data do not change once they are entered into the warehouse.

Data warehouses differ from transactional databases, which contain only raw data and are not designed for queries, reports, or analyses. Therefore, it takes considerable time for a transactional database to perform these tasks. Transactional databases do not store historic data that are necessary for data analyses. Different databases may use different units of measurement for the same attributes, thus making it difficult to perform comparisons.

By contrast, a data warehouse is an analytical database that is used as the foundation of a decision support system. In it, users can explore data, run ad hoc queries, and drill down for details at will. Hence whereas transactional systems are designed to input up-to-the minute data into a database quickly, safely, and efficiently, data warehouses contain information as of a specific point in time and across several functional areas. A data warehouse typically consolidates data from several transactional databases with a time span over several years to enable users to make better decisions by analyzing summarized snapshots of an organization's performance.

Data warehousing is one of the fastest-growing client-server applications. It builds on data architecture, networks, GUI, and relational databases. The four-step development process is very expensive and complex:

1. Extract, model, and assemble data from the operational systems.
2. Transform operational data to a user-focused view.
3. Distribute and manage data changes to the warehouse.
4. Provide access to the data through decision support (DSS) or executive information system (EIS) tools.

Data warehousing has become very popular among organizations seeking competitive advantage by getting strategic information fast and easily. Several industry surveys showed that most of Fortune 500 companies have undertaken some form of data warehousing projects. Although many areas in an organization can benefit from data warehousing, the most promising have been finance, sales analysis, marketing, customer profiling, and market segmentation. Data warehousing consolidates a company's data resource, making it both useful and accessible.

The value of data warehousing is its ability to support decision making and analyses. Internet-based DSS and EIS can be built on data warehouses to support distributed decision processes. A growing number of tools are available, including spreadsheets, desktop databases, report writers, on-line analytical processing (OLAP) tools, and multidimensional database systems. Web-based multidimensional on-line analytical processing (MOLAP) systems are new technologies that enable users to view summary data by zooming in on details by column, by row, or by cell displayed on multilayer spreadsheets. For example, an executive could view summarized sales data for a division by market or by product line. The same executive could also zoom in to view the detailed performance data of a sales group or even a salesperson for a specific product in a specific market. This "slice and dice" capability enables users to examine data horizontally and vertically thanks to its warehousing of data from multiple sources. In a networked environment, this means that decision makers can link forecasting with operational data in a dynamic manner. Changes in aggregated performance data can be traced back to unit-level productivity.

Relevance to Higher Education. A foundation of quality data for decision making is important to higher education, particularly in the area of enrollment management and resource planning. The corporate sector relies on database marketing that uses analytical databases to aid marketing decisions. In higher education, areas that traditionally have consistent data and sound data stewardship, such as finance, may not see the immediate benefits of data warehousing. However, areas that involve complex and distributed decision making, such as budget management or student enrollment and retention, are candidates for data warehousing efforts. Data in these areas can be analyzed from many perspectives. This is especially important because most information systems operations do not have sufficient staff to support on-demand ad hoc queries if the operational systems reside on the mainframe.

How data warehousing in higher education has evolved over the past five years can be illustrated in the following examples:

• Arizona State University (ASU) took three years to consolidate student, financial, and human resource data into an integrated data warehouse (Porter and Rome, 1995). In building the data warehouse, they focused on the strategic needs of information, how frequently data should be updated, and the definition of official data to establish cutoff dates for measuring data spanned over ten years. Policies were established to promote sound data management to ensure that data administrators at the department level are responsible for data integrity. They established consistent measures across several high-level subjects, such as fiscal year, semester or term, department, course, a person's unique ID, and account number, to allow for the integration of different operational systems.

• Ferris State University developed a data warehouse application to deliver timely, accurate student information to college-specific customers (Fisher, 1995). This data warehouse served academic users by providing a PC database environment for working with legacy data. It extended the usefulness of the mainframe-based student information system, which presents information on an individual student basis. The data warehouse enabled academic users to design and create reports and queries by college, department, course, or adviser. The user's ability to customize his or her own queries and reports ultimately led to improved service to students.

• Pennsylvania State University used Web technology to build an EIS to provide summary information for executives, using data automatically extracted from a data warehouse. This EIS operated on the Microsoft SQL server and presented with the Cognos PowerPlay Server Web Edition. These multidimensional information displays are presented in an easy-to-use format over the Web (Pennsylvania State University Executive Information System Coordinating Committee, 1998).

As these examples illustrate, many tools are available to make data warehouses into EIS and DSS. The challenge remains in managing the culture change. Data warehousing involves setting an institutional commitment that data are corporate resources. New policies need to be put in place to ensure sound data management practices. For example, ASU instituted policies to ensure employee access to the administrative data systems while guarding the security of university data. It also implemented data integrity and integration policies to manage university data as an institutional asset, which is represented in a single logical data model that feeds into multiple applications.

Compared to ERP, data warehousing used in conjunction with Web technologies may be a more practical approach to providing sound management data for higher education. Most institutions will not have the resources to migrate to ERP packages in the near future. Web-based data warehousing will provide a cost-effective short-term solution for decision support. For institutions that have adopted or will adopt ERP solutions, most of the ERP software packages are still weak in providing decision support. Additional tools are needed to interface with the ERP software to extract data for warehousing purposes.

Implications for IR. Data warehousing is not a new concept for IR. For many years, IR offices had to extract files from operational databases, such as term enrollment data, to create a longitudinal database for reporting and analyses. The current trend in data warehousing provides a more structured methodology and better technology to augment an old concept. This means that IR offices must develop a solid understanding of the data modeling methodology, relational database technology, and new OLAP and MOLAP tools. More important, data warehousing shifts and distributes analytical responsibility from a central IR office to decision makers in departments, colleges, and administrative offices. This shift means that an IR office should take a leadership role in designing EIS, DSS and data warehouses, shaping polices for data management, and coordinating user training. Examples of data warehousing projects are described in Chapter Three.

A closer working relationship with the information systems area and data managers in departments and colleges will also be necessary. Equipped with the new analytical tools and technologies, IR offices can, in a more timely manner, provide in-depth analysis and reports that integrate multiple data sets spanning colleges, departments, or student cohorts. IR offices will therefore help tie college- and department-level performance data more directly to executive decisions.

Electronic Commerce

Electronic commerce is a broad concept covering three categories of Internet-based activities: Internet, intranet, and extranet. All three types are built on Internet and Web technologies.

Consumer-oriented Internet commerce is in an early stage of formation. This is the model for virtual stores, like amazon.com, and extensions of traditional stores, like Barnes and Noble, or new forms of intermediaries between traditional service providers and customers, like Microsoft Expedia (www.expedia.msn.com). The pervasiveness of the Internet and the ease of use of such technology fuel public interest in this form of electronic commerce. The Web, as an interactive medium, has altered the relationship between the consumer and the service or product providers. Consumers can compare prices and search for products more efficiently on the Web than in the traditional commerce environment. The service and product supply chain is moving toward a more customer-centered model. Successful models are measured not only in financial results but also by their ability to build consumer trust and a virtual community.

Intranets constitute the second form of electronic commerce. These networks are behind corporate firewalls, accessible only by authorized users. They are built on common browsers and corporate network infrastructure and are becoming the platforms for distributing information, sharing knowledge, delivering services, and collaborating between groups. Web technology is easy to learn and use and has standard features. This has made intranets a cost-effective way to extend the life span of aging legacy systems by adding small Web applications to collect and distribute information, such as an update of employee records. Web-based tools could also be used to allow users to query data warehouses through browsers on the intranets.

These approaches are particularly relevant to organizations that do not have resources to adopt ERP systems or move to a new technology platform but have workable databases on the legacy systems. All major ERP vendors are providing software with Web features. Intranets are also ideal for knowledge management because the Web is a collaborative medium.

Extranets are systems for supporting business-to-business electronic commerce. These networks are proprietary, accessible only among partnering organizations. Organizations have used electronic data interchange (EDI) for sharing transaction data about orders, inventories, and delivery, particularly in the auto and retail industries. These data exchanges are limited to transactional data for orders, invoices, and payments. By combining Internet technology with EDI, organizations are able to share data more widely because the technology is readily available and data communications are less costly. The real gain of extranet applications comes from realigning business processes between two organizations, to simplify data exchange and workflow.

The strategic goal of electronic commerce is to integrate the processes supported by extranets, intranets, and the public Internet as a seamless chain of processes. FedEx, as an example, has deployed this strategy by using intranets to link geographically dispersed operations. Its extranet allows companies to manage logistics of delivery and warehousing through FedEx. It links with consumers with online tracking information. In this highly integrated environment, organization boundaries are replaced by customer-centered information flow. However, this integration requires streamlining the work process, data sharing, and a culture of service orientation.

Relevance to Higher Education. Electronic commerce is highly relevant to higher education. The following examples illustrate its applicability:

• Confronted by increased customer demands, rapidly changing technology, and diminishing margins, the Massachusetts Institute of Technology (MIT) chose to reengineer its computer resale store and replaced it with an on-line service that enables students, faculty, and staff to purchase computers, peripherals, and software through a World Wide Web interface. The next phase of the project will generate requisitions through MIT's financial system and process orders and invoices via the Internet through electronic data interchange with the project's local vendor partner (Hallisey, 1998).

• East Carolina University (ECU) implemented new applications for the electronic transfer of student financial aid funds and loan applications (Maclag, 1997). A CommonLine Network and LineSS software enabled the financial aid office to submit electronic loan applications to lenders for processing. The lenders send the university electronic status files, which ECU uses to update the student database and LineSS files. Rosters are processed and funds are automatically credited to each student's account receivable. All charges to the university are paid electronically, and an excess aid check is printed for students whose financial aid exceeds their charges.

Of the three modes of electronic commerce, intranets are most widely adopted by universities and colleges. The Web has quickly transformed electronic collaboration and work processes and has extended the life of legacy systems; for example:

• I have been using the Web as pedagogy for facilitating student project collaboration with project teams as well as between two different classes. HyperNews discussion groups were set up for sharing ideas and for virtual teamwork. Team members posted their project reports in HyperNews designated specifically for each team. Students from a separate class, acting as consultants to team projects, were able to critique these ideas through e-mail, Web posting, and HyperNews discussion. This collaboration extends student learning across two classes. The quality of student projects is significantly improved, as is their satisfaction with the learning experience (Chan and Wolfe, 1999).

• DePaul University's School of Computer Science, Telecommunications, and Information Systems (CTI) recently implemented a rich set of intranet applications to meet student needs. This system allows students to schedule advising appointments with faculty, register for courses, and submit scholarship application forms. Faculty members can access the system to review advisees' academic records, set up schedules, and record advising results. These intranet applications have improved the workflow, bringing faculty and students into direct communication. In addition, distributed learning technology allows for the taping of instruction for Web broadcasting for distance learning, and the administering of assessment tests all through the Web (for an additional discussion of distant learning issues, see Chapter Four).

• Many universities have built small Web applications as the GUI interface with legacy systems. Typical examples are on-line registration, on-line grading, changes to personnel demographic profiles, and budget preparation. These applications can be built incrementally to allow gradual user acceptance.

These applications share a common goal of meeting user needs, particularly student needs. The principles of electronic commerce—streamlining process, reducing demand on user time, building trust with the user community, and making users self-reliant—are applicable in the academy. Student consumerism will demand that institutions deliver services through the Web. Universities and colleges can also create opportunities for partnership with external constituencies, such as alumni and communities.

Implications for IR. Intranets certainly offer IR offices an effective platform for creating and distributing information, as discussed in the sections on knowledge management and data warehousing. In addition, electronic commerce applications raise new issues for IR. Rising consumerism suggests that students, alumni, and even the general public will expect to do business with universities and colleges via the Internet—they will expect to be able to register, apply for financial aid, have loans processed, purchase books and tickets, and obtain instructions on demand. IR must include these issues in needs assessment, satisfaction surveys, and other typical instruments.

Another important issue is the nature of the bond between the institution and its multiple constituent groups. These applications connect directly with students, alumni, and other users, without the involvement of the bursar or other administrators or staffs. How these constituents build relationships with the institution is an emerging issue, as the university becomes more virtual. The positive aspect of this relationship is to attain greater satisfaction among these constituent groups because they can access services and information more efficiently, anytime, anywhere. Poorly executed workflow and information presentation may lead to fragmented loyalty and a tattered institutional image. Thus relationship building in this way has relevance for a wide spectrum of institutional functions, including recruiting, retention, and alumni relations. If these applications secure strong trust among the user groups, IR offices have a special opportunity to collect in-depth data that can augment the existing student information databases.

Conclusions

Knowledge management, enterprise resource planning, data warehousing, and electronic commerce are emerging trends in the corporate sector that have implications for higher education and the IR office. Taken together, these four technology-driven approaches share the following common characteristics.

Transforming Effect. All four approaches have a transforming effect on the academy. These transformations may take several forms. The workflow of administrative and support functions, ranging from human resources record management to academic advising, can be dramatically enhanced by these new approaches. New models for service delivery are emerging to emphasize self-service and the user-driven process chain. Employees can request and receive training on demand. Students can initiate a degree audit and monitor academic process. In addition, new models for instruction leverage communications technologies to support a learner-centered environment. Students can work in virtual teams without time and geographical constraints. The ability to share information and knowledge across institutional boundaries accentuates the importance of collaboration and team problem solving. The capacities of the technology are driven down to the user, enabling greater client-centered access and use of information.

With these technology supports, IR offices will work differently with their institutions and across institutions. They will reach a broader base of user groups through efficient sharing of information and efficient analytical tools. They can form new alliance with librarians, information systems groups, and professional colleagues in creating new data sets and knowledge systems. They can also improve decision making and planning by using their flexible tools for analyzing data at both strategic and operational levels.

To realize these transformations, the implementation of each approach requires a significant change of culture and a redesign of workflow. Of the four, data warehousing is the most limited in scope and therefore the least risky. Electronic commerce applications demand a focus on users. Among the four approaches, it is easiest to establish measurable goals and required process change for electronic commerce. In contrast, knowledge management holds many promises, but the rigid management processes of knowledge creation and distribution and a formal knowledge management system that ties to incentives will not be practical for higher education. Informal knowledge networks could be implemented as intranet applications, which are not difficult to build but may have limited benefits. ERP is most risky for its demand on software-driven process and organization reengineering.

Infrastructure Support. All four approaches are built on the assumption of robust data communication networks, or infrastructure. Institutions need to adopt a broader definition of infrastructure that includes standardization of hardware and software, data policies, Internet and Web browsers, groupware, user training, and support from the information systems group. This broad definition helps institutions gauge their capability and readiness in launching technology-driven transformations. Institutions that do not have a mature technology infrastructure and capabilities will likely experience difficulties in implementing these approaches. In implementing these infrastructure components, IR offices play a pivotal role in designing the data architecture and data policies.

Internet and Web Technology. The Internet has become the ultimate client-server platform because of its ease of use and low costs. All four approaches are converging on the Internet as a set of interrelated solutions. Institutions should focus their investment on user training, standardization of collaborative tools, and policies to guide content management on the Web. IR offices should leverage these technologies for capturing data and distributing information.

New Skills and Roles for IR. Adoption of these approaches means that IR offices need to develop core competencies in five areas:

• *Technical skills.* IR offices should develop expertise in developing Web sites and Web applications. These Web development efforts should result in effective content organization, user interfaces, and database connection. Proficiency in using groupware, such as Lotus Notes, and relational database technology will be necessary skill sets.

• *Process skills.* IR offices need to learn techniques and modeling tools for workflow analysis and process reengineering. Facilitation skills will be essential in developing data policies and process-driven applications. These initiatives demand rigorous change management.

• *Analytical skills.* IR offices have to build new analytical skills for knowledge management and organization analysis. These new dimensions of analyses require insights and broad perspectives about organization process and dynamics.

• *Interpretation skills.* IR offices must develop a strategic outlook to redefine academic process through the rich data sets and highly interactive relationships with a broader user base. Interpretation skills demand a more involved and proactive posture of IR offices.

• *Relationship skills.* Ability to manage on-demand relationships with new internal and external constituencies in a virtual workplace is a key to successful IR support. An IR office needs to map out its services, data sources, and delivery modes against a solid understanding of its roles in transforming the institution and its many constituencies.

In conclusion, the four approaches reviewed in this chapter present new challenges and opportunities for IR professionals, who must redefine their roles and capacities in supporting these technology-driven transformations. Those who expand their skill sets and step into the center of this dynamic process will spur the transformation of their institutions.

References

Chan, S. S., and Wolfe, R. J. "Collaborative Team Learning Approach for Web Development." Paper presented at the 1999 Americas Conference on Information Systems, Milwaukee, Wisconsin, Aug. 13–15, 1999.

Davenport, T. H. "Putting the Enterprise into the Enterprise System." *Harvard Business Review,* July–Aug. 1998, 121–131.

Davenport, T. H., and Prusak, L. *Working Knowledge: How Organizations Manage What They Know.* Boston: Harvard Business School Press, 1998.

Fisher, L. "Data Warehousing Puts New Life into Legacy System." Paper presented at the CAUSE Conference, New Orleans, Dec. 1995.

Foster, L. A., and Herndon, B. T. "Implementation of Reengineered Procurement Process at Duke University, Using Technology and Work Process Redesign." Paper presented at the CAUSE Conference, Minneapolis, Minn., Dec. 1997.

Gage, J. F. "Making PeopleSoft Administrative Systems Work: The Case for Business Process Redesign." Paper presented at the CAUSE Conference, Orlando, Fla., Dec. 1998.

Hallisey, J. "Riding the Crest of the E-Commerce Wave: Transforming MIT's Campus Computer Resale Operation." *CAUSE/EFFECT,* 1998, *21* (2), 51–52, 58.

Maclag, L. S. "Electronic Transfer of Financial Aid Funds and Loan Applications (Using the CommonLine Network)." Paper presented at the College and University Computer Users Association Annual Conference, St. Louis, Mo., May 1997.

Nelson, K. R., and Scoby, J. L. "Implementing Decentralized Responsibility-Centered Management with Budget Restructuring and Cutting Edge Technologies." Paper presented at the CAUSE Conference, Orlando, Fla., Dec. 1998.

Oblinger, D. G., and Verville, A. "Information Technology as a Change Agent." *Educom Review,* 1999, *34* (1), 46–55.

Pennsylvania State University Executive Information System Coordinating Committee. "Building Information out of Data: Executive Information System at Penn State." Paper presented at the CAUSE Conference, Orlando, Fla., Dec. 1998.

Porter, J. D., and Rome, J. J. "Lessons from a Successful Data Warehouse Implementation." *CAUSE/EFFECT,* 1995, *18* (4), 43–50.

SUSY S. CHAN is associate professor and director of the Information Systems Division and the Institute for Electronic Commerce at the School of Computer Science, Telecommunications, and Information Systems at DePaul University. She has served as vice president for information technology and vice president for planning at DePaul.

2

Advances in technology have increased access to informa-
tion both on and off the campus. Open access, coupled
with pressures for accountability, has brought new chal-
lenges to the IR office.

Accountability, Technology, and External Access to Information: Implications for IR

Joan Wells, Elizabeth Silk, David Torres

Information technology is rapidly and fundamentally altering the flow of information within and across economies, institutions, and cultures. The amount of information available and the speed at which it may be obtained and analyzed is astounding. Whether communication and knowledge are enhanced is, of course, debatable. However, it is clear that change of this magnitude and pace can be likened in historical terms to the industrial revolution. It promises to change the way we work, live, and interact in very fundamental ways.

Education, a knowledge-based industry, is one of the workplaces directly affected and challenged by advances in information technology. These advances directly influence the way information and knowledge are gathered, analyzed, and communicated. Institutional researchers process a vast array of data to support decision-making, planning, and policy formulation (Delaney, 1997). They are therefore among the most profoundly affected by this technological change.

Concurrent with technological change has been the emergence of a policy environment in which publicly funded colleges and universities face new demands to be accountable to legislative and oversight agencies. Over the past decade, public service providers have eliminated services, diversified funding, adopted alternative service provision arrangements, and focused on improving performance. Broadly labeled rethinking or "reinventing government" (Osborne and Gaebler, 1992), reinvention embraces notions of entrepreneurial, customer-driven management (Gore, 1994; Advisory

Commission for Intergovernmental Relations, 1987). Entrepreneurial, customer-driven organizations "learn to offer choices, establish accountability and finance themselves" ("Reinventing Government," 1995, p. 151). Institutional researchers are called on to support college efforts to become student-centered, respond to calls for greater accountability, and seek alternative funding sources.

Demands for greater accountability create greater demands for institutional information. Advances in information technology continually provide greater access to data and enhanced tools for analysis. As a result, researchers are both aided and challenged by an expanding array of internal and external data to be analyzed to inform decision making. Taken together, advances in information technology and the changing relationship between institutions of higher education and their legislative, governing, regulatory, and funding bodies have altered the nature and scope of institutional research.

Changing Access to Information

Sanford (1995) states that access to information is the key component of the profound change under way in institutional research. Advances in computing hardware and software, the expansion of the use of local area networks linked to campuswide networks, and the Internet have expanded access to information for both on- and off-campus users. These advances have changed the scope of research projects, the way reports and services are produced, and the range of formats used to communicate findings.

The Transition from Mainframe to Client-Server Systems. Many colleges are shifting away from what was once the standard mainframe environment to one that is client-server based. As described in Chapter One, these new systems provide comprehensive database resources using decentralized information storage units. Although a certain degree of end-user access is possible in mainframe environments, data retrieval is often conducted indirectly, requiring assistance and special programming from the central data processing department. In contrast, client-server systems have the capacity to provide immediate and direct access to information to a wide range of campus constituents.

In his overview of advances in information technology during the latter part of the twentieth century, Thomas (1995) observes that the expansion of data access, along with the increased storage capacity for historical data, will provide the tools needed for institutional researchers to produce the in-depth analyses needed for decision making. Projects that involve processing extensive amounts of information can now be conducted without disruption of essential data functions. Institutional databases (financial aid, student characteristics and enrollment, alumni, and other areas), which often exist separately on mainframe systems, can function as parts of a whole on a networked system. This expanded coordination of campus data is of great benefit to institutional researchers as they are called to respond to a widening range of research and planning questions requiring an integrated understanding of college management. For example, student characteristics, enrollment, and faculty workload data can be integrated with facilities data to inform facilities planning. Alumni data can be evaluated to make better sense of student outcomes. Another example would be a study on economic disadvantage and the impact of financial aid on student success. Although many of these types of studies could be conducted using the older approach, the integration of institutional systems decreases the time and human resource commitment that made them prohibitive in the past.

The benefits of evolving information technology are, however, unevenly experienced by institutional researchers. Potentially, client-server database systems may be housed in decentralized campus locations and support decentralized access. In practice, systems continue to be managed and controlled by a central department or entity whose name may reflect the history of information management at an institution (data processing, computing services, or information technology). Regardless of name, these central entities establish access protocols so that the majority of campus members have restricted access to information. Such control is imperative to ensure data integrity and maintain the privacy rights of students.

Furthermore, many campuses are years away from acquiring the resources to develop a client-server-based information management system. The cost of this transformation can be formidable, and the process can be long and arduous. Many of the newer database system packages available to private industry are still relatively untried in academic settings. Nevertheless, as more networked systems are developed, implementation timelines and costs should decrease. Even at institutions without new networked systems, the expansion of desktop computer capacity and the accessibility of global networks greatly enhance local data retrieval and analysis.

Expanded Access to External Data Sources. Technology is not only streamlining access to internal information systems but also expanding access to data outside the institution. Since the expansion of the Internet, external data sources have become more numerous and easier to retrieve and manipulate locally. Increasingly, Web designs are database-driven. Sites can be established to collect as well as distribute information and data. Ever-expanding computing power supports the creation of databases built by downloading, merging, and manipulating data across departments, institutions, and agencies. (Schaefer and Massa explore these capacities in Chapter Three.) Software products ranging from familiar statistical packages like SPSS and SAS to PC-based querying software enhance our ability to view and analyze data and to communicate information to IR's many clients. For example, demographic information can be accessed quickly through FEDSTATS or state agency or private provider Web sites and displayed by ZIP code, tract, or block using GIS or mapping software to illustrate trends within a college's catchment area.

Examination of state and federal educational data for comparison and benchmarking purposes is not new to higher education (Lenth, 1991).

National data on higher education have been available to institutional researchers for years, but over the past decade, revolutionary changes in information technology have allowed various state and federal agencies to increase accessibility. Many, if not most, state and federal government agencies now distribute public data via the Internet. The Compendium of National Data Sources on Higher Education, produced by the organization of State Higher Education Executive Officers (SHEEO), provides one of the most comprehensive guides to these resources.

Other public and private organizations also offer useful data, but rarely free of charge. For example, the National Student Loan Clearinghouse, in addition to offering financial aid services, can provide information to institutions concerning the educational activities of students after program completion or separation. In exchange for this service, called TransferTrack, the Clearinghouse requests a small fee and access to student data. TransferTrack is attractive to many institutions because it provides extensive information on students' enrollment activities at both private and public institutions throughout the country, information that has heretofore been unavailable. Data are also available from testing agencies, such as ACT, that have begun to offer a range of research services to colleges and universities. In exchange for student data, ACT offers the Freshman Class Profile Service, which contains summary information about the characteristics and academic abilities of incoming students.

For years, many IR professionals have contemplated the profound impact sharing data resources with other governmental agencies could have on their efforts to provide comprehensive and accurate findings on student outcomes. Data from agencies such as the Internal Revenue Service, the Social Security Administration, and from the unemployment insurance wage were inaccessible due to issues concerning security, privacy, turf and control, and the sheer volume and complexity of the data. In recent years, a few states and college districts have forged agreements with state agencies of employment to gain access to their data. The California community college system is one of the first higher education entities to assess the feasibility of using wage data to study postcollegiate employment rates and wages. Studies have documented the positive impact a community college education has on earnings (Sanchez and Laanan, 1998).

The Promise of Access. Advances in technology are reconfiguring information access both on and off the campus. Streamlined access to institutional information can provide the institutional researcher with the capacity to address research and planning issues from a more integrated systems perspective. At the same time, it portends substantial institutional change, requiring renewed discussions concerning issues of confidentiality and interpretation.

Access to the growing number of external data sources can be both exciting and overwhelming for institutional research professionals. These data provide opportunities to explore policy issues at a level that was unachievable in the past. Nevertheless, each data resource has its strengths and limitations, and these should be examined thoroughly prior to institutional commitment of financial and human resources toward their acquisition and development.

The implications of access for the changing role of institutional research are conditioned by the policy context in which greater access has emerged. For this reason, the ramifications of greater access will be discussed following a discussion of the demands for information embedded in the accountability movement. Institutional researchers are gaining greater access to information as a result of technological change as the need for reporting and understanding educational outcomes grows.

Reinventing Educational Service Provision

New trends in information technology have affected all professionals in fields involving the gathering, manipulation, and communication of information. Yet the IT revolution alone does not account for the expansion and diversification of the roles institutional research plays in higher education. It is the influence of changing technology, combined with a shift in the relationship between higher education and its external constituents, that has led many institutions to rely on their IR departments to inform an increasingly demanding policy agenda.

Under the Microscope. The accountability movement in higher education is representative of a general trend in government service provision. As in many policy areas, there has been a shift away from entitlement funding. Declining public trust, competitive budgetary processes, the emergence of "middle class" suburban politics, and the devolution of the federal role in intergovernmental relations back to the states are reflected in the current consumer-based, outcome-driven public sector environment. No longer are funds appropriated for higher education assured; states are now demanding evidence that colleges and universities are delivering "purchased" services and anticipated outcomes, that is, that they are meeting the needs of the state (Albright, 1998). The performance monitoring and benchmarking processes advocated in calls for government reinvention have taken the form of school report cards and institutional effectiveness reporting. As a result, educational institutions are required to produce and report quality, effectiveness, and productivity measures to a greater extent each year.

One measure of the pervasiveness of this trend is the number of states that have adopted performance-based systems of funding over the past decade. According to a recent study conducted by Christal (1998) for SHEEO, thirty-seven states use performance indicators of colleges and universities to some extent. Twenty-three states indicated that they use the information to inform the public about institutional performance, and the same number have linked the measures to funding. If current trends persist, a greater number of states will adopt funding models linked to performance. In general, only a small portion of state budgets are connected to performance (between 0.5 and 4 percent), but as states gain more experience with these types of allocation practices, the figures may increase. In South Carolina, 100 percent of all higher education funding will be allocated according to performance, starting in the year 2000.

Customer-Centered Focus. Performance funding flows from a conceptualization of the budgeting authority, often state government, as the consumer of higher education services. Increasingly, budgeting decisions reflect a purchase of service perspective. States, as consumers of higher education services, expect that educational needs are being met in return for budget allocations (Albright, 1998). Performance and outcome reports determine how well the expected services were delivered.

Other legislation focuses on the consumer rights of individual students. Illustrative of this trend is the federal Student Right to Know mandate that colleges and universities publish their graduation rates for first-time degree-seeking students. The legislation reflects frustration with the increase in student time required to earn a degree. Rates are based on definitions contained in the Interdisciplinary Postsecondary Education Data System (IPEDS) Graduation Rate Survey and reflect the percentage of students in each identified cohort completing their program within 150 percent of normal time. Beginning in January 2000, graduation rates must be disclosed or published in college brochures, catalogues, schedules, and other literature supplied to students and to anyone planning to enter into a financial relationship with the institution.

Since comparable public information is collected from all colleges and universities, institutions can anticipate being ranked by graduation rate. Such rankings are thought to provide the education consumer with data for more informed enrollment choices. Graduation rates do not, however, adequately represent or inform the growing percentage of students in adult markets who may attend college for retraining or career advancement rather than to obtain a degree.

Similarly, accrediting agencies and commissions have emphasized institutional effectiveness in the self-study structure. For example, the Western Association of Schools and Colleges (WASC) added a standard that deals solely with effectiveness. An institutional research professional is assigned to each visiting team to assist in the accreditation process. Also focused on institutional effectiveness, the North Central Association of Colleges and Schools (NCA) has required that its institutions develop assessment programs that document student academic achievement for almost a decade. Taken together, these programs are designed to build internal feedback loops that are intended to improve the quality of teaching and learning and produce evidence that the institution can strengthen its educational effectiveness.

Alternative Funding Sources. Limited budgets have fueled the search for alternative and diversified funding sources. Increasingly, colleges turn to state, federal, and private grants to support activities. Reporting criteria are outcome or results-oriented.

On the national level, the federal Government Performance and Results Act requires that institutions receiving federal funding develop and report performance indicators. Another example is the Workforce Investment Act (WIA) of 1998 (Public Law 105-220), which is a major effort to reform and restructure workforce development programs throughout the country that will take effect on July 1, 2000. It replaces the Job Training Partnership Act (JTPA) and several other federal laws that support programs that fund workforce development projects in an attempt to consolidate and reduce the bureaucratic layers involved in the myriad of existing programs.

The WIA involves millions of training and education dollars that sustain occupational programs at colleges and other organizations. One of the provisions of the WIA calls for a performance accountability system at both the state and local levels. The core indicators of performance outlined by the WIA are enrollment, attainment of recognized credentials, placement rates, employment retention rates, and earnings. Many states have chosen to link WIA funding allocations to performance levels (National Association of Private Industry Councils, 1998).

The demand for performance accountability and consumer-oriented information by key external constituents has forced postsecondary institutions to establish reporting systems that can generate this information. The pressure to respond to these mandates has grown as key funding streams are increasingly linked to performance-based formulas and threaten the financial health of our institutions. Establishing the data systems and reporting structure necessary to provide this information has fallen primarily on IR offices.

Together, changing technology and greater accountability are shaping the demands and roles performed by institutional researchers and institutional research departments. The interplay of these trends is apparent in the emergence of two developments in institutional research. The first is revealed in the evolution of the IR office and the role or function the office performs in each institution. A new role is emerging in which researchers take the lead in linking their institutions with the information required for decision making. The second development flows from the ability of third parties to influence the institutional research agenda. Both developments are changing the way we do business.

Changing the Way We Do Business

Information technology has changed the rules of work for all information-based professionals. All must adapt to new demands and methods of performing tasks, from the most basic to the most complex. For institutional researchers, this has meant yet another stage in the evolution of the profession and its role in the information infrastructure of postsecondary institutions. Advances in information technology permit greater access to and dissemination of data. At the same time, the demand for information seems to be expanding exponentially. College constituencies increasingly look to institutional researchers to guide them through the maze of data resources and to convert data into information for decision making. The IR office has moved beyond basic reporting functions to play a critical role within the informational infrastructure of colleges.

The Evolution of Institutional Research Roles. Institutional research is a comparatively young profession. Indeed, many colleges do not yet have IR offices. In such environments, institutional research is often performed by faculty or other consultants. At the other extreme, colleges support offices providing a wide range of services, from reporting to policy analysis and advocacy. This progression of services or roles has been classified into three functional emphases: description, understanding, and advocacy (Claggett, 1996). The most basic function performed by IR offices is descriptive. Activities include data collection and presentation character- ized by college factbooks, external reporting, and request-driven reports. Building on this function, IR offices raise questions and conduct analyses to clarify trends noted in descriptive reports. Finally, IR offices acquire con- textual awareness and expertise and are integrated in the executive decision- making structures of the college. Claggett (1996) notes, "Implications for institutional research practice include reorienting the research time frame to meet internal and external data to provide contextual understanding, broadening office expertise into new areas such as institutional advance- ment, and emphasizing issue-oriented integration and synthesis of findings from multiple projects rather than detailed presentations focusing on indi- vidual studies (Chan and Smith, 1991). Increasingly, the institutional researcher is becoming involved in institutional advocacy."

Similarly, Terenzini (1991) challenges institutional researchers to add issue and contextual intelligence to their strengths. He conceptualizes this evolution of roles as reflecting three forms of organizational intelligence: technical/analytical intelligence, issues intelligence, and contextual intelli- gence.

1. *Technical/analytical intelligence* refers to the fundamental technical com- petencies, which must be embodied in all institutional research offices. Professionals must be competent in database development; research design and methods; mainframe and personal computing; and oral and written communication.

2. *Issues intelligence* requires understanding the substantive problems, orga- nizational procedures, and political character of our client base so that research can play a meaningful role in decision making.

3. *Contextual intelligence* embodies the human relations and analytical skills required to understand organizational cultures and environmental con- texts. It "optimizes the effective application of technical competencies and issues awareness to a particular institution and its problem" (Claggett, 1996). It is the form of intelligence that earns institutional research and researchers legitimacy, trust, and respect.

Both Claggett and Terenzini observe that information technologies and demands for greater institutional accountability are driving the evolution of the institutional research office. Both also encourage institutional researchers to assume a proactive role in shaping the organizational intelligence of their institutions. Researchers are uniquely positioned to design the linkages among data, information, and decision makers. In essence, institutional researchers are encouraged to become information architects.

Figure 2.1 presents an integration of both conceptualizations of IR and the emerging role of the information architect in the form of a continuum. The continuum can be viewed as a timeline mapping the evolution of the many roles and products of institutional research offices. Above the timeline are the roles that have been assumed by institutional research offices. Listed beneath the timeline are examples of activities and publications to be expected from offices performing each role or function. At the left end of the continuum are the earliest evolving roles and products. Included are descriptive reports on student enrollment and trend reports on many of the same indicators embodied in factbook data presentations. Moving to the right along the continuum, roles and tasks become more complex. The newest and most complex role, information architect, requires the acquisition of Terenzini's contextual intelligence and an understanding of the potential of emerging technologies. The architect must understand the informational needs of the organization and design an infrastructure supportive of expanded access to information and enhanced understanding.

Progression along the continuum does not eliminate earlier functions. Offices must still meet basic reporting functions as they develop the capacity to perform more analytical and contextual roles. Clearly, technological advances can inform and facilitate the functions performed at each step of this continuum. However, as described by other authors in this volume, the dramatic forces of information access and accountability drive this evolution forward. The following discussion illustrates the dynamic nature of the interplay between these two forces and the consequences it is having on the evolution of institutional research.

Traditional Roles Revisited. The forces of access and accountability have substantial implications for traditional IR activities. As reporters and interpreters of data, researchers must rethink established, previously routinized procedures as technology increases the ability of on-campus users to access information and generate reports customized to their needs. This process is discussed in full in Chapter Three using two case studies to illustrate the capacities of current information technologies. The realities of on-demand access and decentralized reporting raise anew issues surrounding the wisdom and legality of open access.

Perhaps most obvious is concern regarding the confidentiality of educational data. Greater care must be taken to ensure that open access does not allow end users to identify or inappropriately report information on individual students or employees. In addition, many users will access data without fully understanding its origin or its meaning. Users may report data

Figure 2.1. The Evolution of Institutional Research Roles

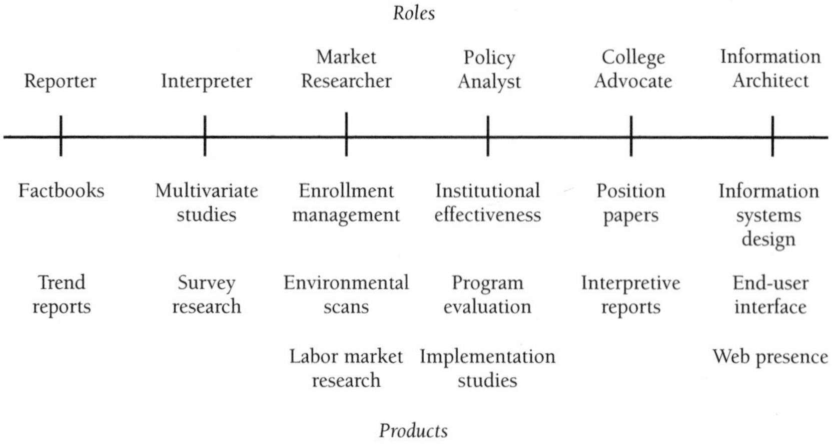

Roles

Reporter	Interpreter	Market Researcher	Policy Analyst	College Advocate	Information Architect
Factbooks	Multivariate studies	Enrollment management	Institutional effectiveness	Position papers	Information systems design
Trend reports	Survey research	Environmental scans	Program evaluation	Interpretive reports	End-user interface
		Labor market research	Implementation studies		Web presence

Products

inaccurately or without providing proper context. Consequently, institutional researchers must move beyond reporting to educating the readership. This involves interpreting, analyzing, and providing contextual relevance to audiences inside and outside the college community. In short, issues and contextual intelligence must be infused into the reporting role.

In their market research and policy analyst roles, institutional researchers must learn how to leverage access to external information most effectively. Researchers must develop a broader interpretive focus. At the same time, pressures for accountability have expanded reporting requirements and increased the number of education policy reports. Colleges often turn to the expertise of the institutional research office to interpret and respond to challenges emanating from state agencies, the press, and other external sources. IR offices are asked to conduct further analyses to buttress college positions before administrative and legislative budgeting and oversight agencies. As a result, researchers must develop issues and contextual intelligences to monitor and understand a wider policy context in order to fulfill the more recently acquired roles of policy analyst and college advocate.

For the institution, the push for greater access, whether through systems modifications, advances in networking, or other technologies, brings with it dislocating institutional change. With change comes the challenge of recovering previously established procedures and capabilities as well as harnessing the promise of these new systems. Institutional researchers are often called on to fill in the gaps in newly designed data management systems. Potentially, the IR architect is part of a team of professionals working together to design, implement, and extend access to information services for the college community.

Emerging Roles of IR. In addition to revisions of traditional IR functions, new roles for IR are emerging. IR professionals are challenged to assist in the design of college informational infrastructures sufficient to translate data into information for decision making and performance monitoring. As suggested earlier, the emergence of the information architect role requires the integration of Terenzini's three forms of organizational intelligence with newly emerging skill sets. Many of these new roles and skill sets are common to many, if not all, attempts to access and communicate information in the information age.

In a recent presentation to the California Community Colleges' Ed>Net Multimedia Entertainment Initiative (MEI) Committee (1999), representatives from the Web design industry discussed workforce development needs. The emergence of the Web design industry was characterized as a meeting of the design and communication worlds with the engineering and computing worlds. This convergence has produced a demand for hybrid professionals who can meet with clients, understand consumer viewpoints, and solve the many design problems of communicating information in the interactive, nonlinear Web-based environment required to conduct electronic commerce on a global scale. These professionals design and map the information structure of Web sites. They must be cognizant of the content and interactivity of Web pages and understand how customers might view, analyze, and interpret information at a client's Web site. They must understand how humans relate to this new technology.

The Web design industry is not unique in its need for such hybrid professionals. Representatives of the computer game, animation, entertainment, and educational software industries have described similar workforce development needs in presentations to the MEI Committee. The presentations of these industry panels repeatedly identify a need for hybrid professionals, well trained in emerging technologies, capable of adapting to technological change, and well educated in the communication arts. This vision of the new technology or the hybrid professional resounds in the writings of Claggett (1996), Terenzini (1991), Lohmann (1998), and many other institutional researchers grappling with the challenges of the information age. Technological competency is insufficient. IR professionals must develop and maintain a keen understanding of policy contexts and the organizational milieus in which they work. This understanding must in turn inform the design of the information infrastructure of the college.

A Foot in Both Worlds. The role of information architect requires the IR professional to maintain the technological expertise to talk knowledgeably with computing professionals. At the same time, to respond effectively to issues of accountability, IR professionals must understand the substantive issue and policy contexts in which their clients, an institution's decision makers, reside. Put bluntly, institutional researchers have their feet in both worlds.

The IR office is uniquely situated in the college organization to link knowledge consumers to the information rapidly emerging as a result of new technologies developed to manage information resources. Researchers often serve on college decision-making bodies and must bring an understanding of client needs to the design of the information infrastructure. As policy analysts and college advocates, IR professionals are profoundly aware of the context of institutional decisions. This awareness cannot help but improve the design of information systems.

In addition, IR offices must often establish new relationships inside and outside their organizational units. Unfortunately, institutional researchers may face organizational impediments in their efforts to influence the information architecture of an institution. It is sometimes difficult to convince centralized computing or information technology departments to invite institutional research into system planning discussions. The placement of the institutional research department in the organizational structure of the college largely determines its degree of influence. For example, in the California community college system, IR departments are found in information services, planning, matriculation and counseling, and even public relations divisions. Though organizational cultures vary, it is likely that offices within the same division will interact more frequently and be more likely to influence information system planning decisions.

Despite such difficulties, IR professionals must cultivate acceptance of their role as information architects. They are uniquely qualified and situated to link managers with the information required for decision making. As technology and the demand for information drive institutional change, researchers will be increasingly asked to support the culture of evidence and assessment called for by accrediting agencies. As information architects, they will be instrumental in the capacity of colleges to meet emerging demands.

Research Agenda Control: Putting Out Fires

One final consequence of the convergence of changing information technology and greater accountability can be observed. New roles and decentralized access to institutional data create a potential "wild card" for the institutional research office. Staff are called on to address reports and findings gleaned by external policy analysts from data posted at innumerable agency Web sites. Often the complicated nature of institutional statistical reporting requires contextual information to appreciate to the fullest the phenomena it is documenting.

For example, the Chancellor's Office of the California Community Colleges has generated the data for Student Right to Know graduation rates by college and for the entire system. This information is currently accessible to California colleges at its Web site and will be made available to the public in January 2000. This cohort of first-time full-time degree-, certificate-, or transfer-seeking students represented 3 percent of the state's community college enrollments in the fall of 1995. However, results will be reported promptly in local newspapers. Journalists and the public at-large may not fully note definitional distinctions and contextual information when interpreting the rates. In anticipation of the mandated public disclosure, institutional research offices throughout the state are preparing reports to provide additional information on Student Right to Know graduation and transfer rates.

Research departments are also asked to confirm data reported by external agencies. For example, given expanded access to data, colleges can now question population growth rates generated by state demographic units. In other cases, researchers must validate information from agencies reporting on higher education. Regardless of whether the source of an error can be traced to the institution or an external agency, verification of data, especially in cases where the institution's effectiveness is questioned, requires a shift in departmental resources.

Clearly, external variables of this nature can disrupt an established research agenda. Resources are reallocated to respond to issues of immediate concern. In the case of graduation rates, rates need not be made public until January 2000. Institutional researchers have time to prepare for public discussion. However, expanded access and rapid data dissemination present the possibility that schedules will be disrupted. The need to respond quickly to serious inquiries becomes a priority.

At the core of these issues of greater data access and decentralization is a loss of institutional control. Agendas are derailed to provide contextual information and understanding. Research offices face the challenge of maintaining a research agenda in the face of overwhelming demands—demands that with technology take on an immediacy that is new to the educational environment.

Widespread dissemination of findings and opportunities affects the human and material resources of the department. As research departments plan their work schedules, determined by internal institutional forces (such as institutional mission statement objectives) and external forces (such as government agency reporting requirements), there is a need to prioritize and allocate work assignments to department members in a manner that ensures quality and efficiency. Priority and staffing decisions must incorporate and recognize the emergence of the policy analyst and advocate roles and the possibility that researchers will be increasingly called on to play these roles.

The potential dislocating effect of "informational wild cards" is illustrated by the accompanying flowcharts. Historically, as shown in Figure 2.2, an institution's data were collected and forwarded to oversight agencies. Concurrently, institutional researchers assembled the data into reports and distributed the reports to interested stakeholders. This was a very labor- and time-intensive proposition, but there was an unforeseen benefit to research departments: it allowed time for institutional analysis and interpretation before the findings were made public.

**Figure 2.2. Model of Institutional Research Dissemination
Without the External Unanticipated Variable**

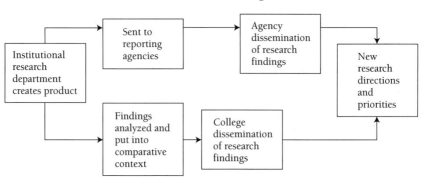

Advances in information technology have changed this. Rapid information dissemination limits the time for analysis and expands the number of
stakeholders who will access the information. Consequently, the institutional
research agenda is disrupted. Figure 2.3 demonstrates the additional time and
resources that are required when the department must address externally generated wild card issues.

The crucial difference is in the amount of time the research department
is given to gather and prepare a report for public viewing. In the new model,
the dissemination of data is almost instantaneous, thereby creating a situation where quick and often inadequate analysis will be conducted by the
third party. This potentially dubious analysis then becomes a catalyst for the
later stages of the model, where valuable research resources are diverted to
address these ad hoc concerns.

Ideally, a compromise between internal reporting concerns and external accountability needs can address both sets of priorities, as shown in Figure 2.4. As external agencies increasingly acknowledge the importance of
gathered institutional data, these agencies need to communicate with the
originating institutions. Clear documentation of edits, measurement, analysis, and reporting formats should be shared as early as possible. Findings
and any corroborating or explanatory materials should be forwarded to colleges and IR offices in advance of public dissemination. This will provide
valuable time to anticipate comments and place the report into a meaningful context for local audiences.

Although this step proposes more work for the reporting agencies, it
will lessen misunderstandings brought about by unanticipated externally
generated informational wild cards. The MIS division of the California Community Colleges is making such an effort. Representatives are traveling
throughout the state, updating researchers, chief instructional officers, and

Figure 2.3. Model of Institutional Research Dissemination with the External Unanticipated Variable

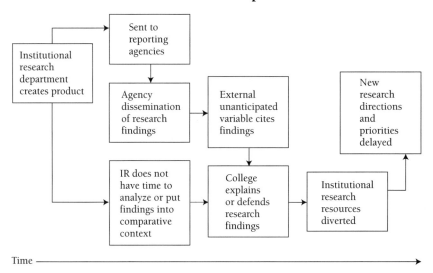

others on reporting requirements, data edits, upcoming reports, and a range of data files, software, and services available to assist colleges in responding to accountability initiatives. Such meetings and conversations foster a feeling of partnership and commitment to a systemwide assessment culture.

Concluding Thoughts

In this chapter, we discussed the dual impact of advancing information technology and increasing demands for institutional accountability. The confluence of the revolutionary changes in information technology and increasing demands for accountability requires expansion of the traditional duties of institutional research and the development of hybrid skill sets.

IR professionals are increasingly called on to bridge the worlds of information technology, policy analysis, and applied research. New responsibilities as data interpreter, college advocate, educator, and information architect involve a broader range of skills and knowledge. Hybrid skills to make use of ever-changing information technologies and to manage, package, and communicate information to many stakeholders and publics are now prerequisites of effective IR offices.

Envisioning the IR professional as an individual with a hybrid skill set or a "jack of all trades" is not new to IR. It is a field in which the professionals involved have traditionally juggled several roles at once. What is new is a different level of responsibility and a heightened sense of urgency. Researchers have always been responsible for analyzing and presenting

**Figure 2.4. Model of Institutional Research Dissemination
with External Agency Cooperation**

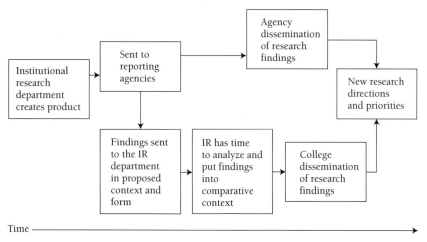

findings in ways that maximize accuracy and policymaking. As information architects, researchers must also contribute to the design of information infrastructures capable of quickly responding to information requests in ways that clearly communicate college goals and contexts.

References

Advisory Commission for Intergovernmental Relations. *The Organization of Local Public Economies.* Washington, D.C.: Advisory Commission for Intergovernmental Relations, 1987.

Albright, B. N. "Performance-Based Funding." *Network News,* 1998, *17* (1), 4–5.

California Community Colleges Ed>Net Multimedia Entertainment Initiative Committee. Web design industry panel discussion, San Francisco, Mar. 5, 1999.

Chan, S. S., and Smith, K. "The Changing Roles of Institutional Research in Strategic Management." Presentation at the Thirty-First Annual Forum of AIR, San Francisco, May 1991.

Christal, M. E. "State Survey on Performance Measures, 1996–97." *Network News,* 1998, *17* (1), 1–3.

Claggett, C. A. "Maximum Impact: Research Strategies for Effective Institutional Management, Assessment, and Advocacy." Presentation at the Annual Summer Institute on Institutional Effectiveness and Student Success, Charleston, S.C., June 1996.

Delaney, M. D. "The Role of Institutional Research in Higher Education." *Research in Higher Education,* 1997, *38* (1), 1–16.

Gore, Al, Jr. *Creating a Government That Works Better and Costs Less.* Washington, D.C.: National Performance Review, 1994.

Lenth, C. S. (ed.). *Using National Databases.* New Directions for Institutional Research, no. 69. San Francisco: Jossey-Bass, 1991.

Lohmann, D. "Positioning IR as a Major Player in Policy Decisions: Problems to Solve, Actions to Take." Paper presented at the forum of the Association for Institutional Research, Minneapolis, Minn., May 1998.

National Association of Private Industry Councils. *The Workforce Investment Act of 1998.* Washington, D.C.: National Association of Private Industry Councils, 1998.

Osborne, D., and Gaebler, T. *Reinventing Government: How the Entrepreneurial Spirit Is Transforming the Public Sector.* Reading, Mass.: Addison-Wesley, 1992.

"Reinventing Government." *CQ Researcher,* 1995, 5 (7), 145–168.

Sanchez, J. R., and Laanan, F. S. "Determining the Economic Benefits of Attending Community College." In A. M. Cohen (ed.), *Determining the Economic Benefits of Attending Community College.* New Directions for Community Colleges, no. 104. San Francisco: Jossey-Bass, 1998.

Sanford, T. R. "Higher Education and Institutional Research: What Lies Ahead." In T. R. Sanford (ed.), *Preparing for the Information Needs of the Twenty-First Century.* New Directions for Higher Education, no. 85. San Francisco: Jossey-Bass, 1995.

Terenzini, P. T. "On the Nature of Institutional Research and the Knowledge and Skills It Requires." Paper presented at the thirty-first forum of the Association for Institutional Research, San Francisco, May 1991.

Thomas, C. R. "Harnessing Information Technology in the Twenty-First Century." In T. R. Sanford (ed.), *Preparing for the Information Needs of the Twenty-First Century.* New Directions for Higher Education, no. 85. San Francisco: Jossey-Bass, 1995.

JOAN WELLS is director of institutional research at Riverside Community College in Riverside, California.

ELIZABETH SILK is assistant dean for research and planning at Harold Washington College, one of the City Colleges of Chicago.

DAVID TORRES is an institutional research specialist and teaches sociology at Riverside Community College in Riverside, California.

3

This chapter presents case studies from Illinois Institute of Technology and Willamette University demonstrating how institutional researchers have harnessed new information technologies to streamline office functions.

The Webs We Weave: The Dynamic IR Office

Ed Schaefer, Tod Massa

Better, faster, cheaper. These three words have been the clarion cry of the technology revolution of the 1990s (not to be confused with the 1890s, which experienced a technology revolution of their own). Technologists, developers, programmers, and vendors have promised all three things—but they have not always delivered. With what seems like monthly spending for software and hardware upgrades, cost overruns, and time lost to retraining, has new technology made IR services cheaper? Faster? Sure, we can process data more quickly, but does this actually speed up the analytical process? As for better, are our answers better? Has technology made our information more useful or simply easier to access? Or have we begun to slip in our attentiveness to focusing on what is most important in favor of more description and detail without adding value?

Regardless of the answers to these questions, administrators and others, both on and off campus, are demanding increasing amounts of data and information. IR offices worldwide are caught between the dynamic tension of greater quantity and greater quality—always with the expectation that the technology provides the capabilities to do more without increasing resources.

The following case studies at small IR offices at Illinois Institute of Technology and Willamette University describe how technology had affected the IR functions of these two offices.

Case Study 1: Illinois Institute of Technology— Using the World Wide Web to Deliver a Central Faculty Database

Illinois Institute of Technology (IIT) is a four-year, private urban university with approximately 300 full-time and 230 part-time faculty and 6,000 students. In 1995, after a yearlong strategic planning process, the institution underwent a major curriculum and organizational reorganization. As part of this, the Office of Information and Institutional Research (OIIR) was set up. Its goal was to provide greater access to high-quality institutional data and act as a central clearinghouse for information requests on campus.

With two full-time staff members, one part-time student assistant, and a formidable charge, OIIR sought to use technology solutions to streamline information management. We believed that information technology solutions would make our information flow more manageable, would improve information request efficiency, and could be implemented within our budget. Unfortunately, what should have been a major resource, our Computing and Network Services department, was not at that time very responsive to the needs of individual university offices. Therefore, much of the development and maintenance of whatever systems were needed fell squarely on this IR office. We were going to strive for faster, cheaper, and better information.

We were quickly put to the task regarding university faculty data. Our two-and-a-half-year odyssey would demonstrate that technology may not improve the quality of data, but it does improve the quality of our office life. Also, the technological hat we chose to wear would not change the goals and missions of this office but would alter our perceptions of an IR office.

Faculty Information Management. One of the first challenges we faced was taming the Hydra we called faculty data, a truly Herculean task. As the myth goes, Hercules tried to defeat the Hydra by cutting off its various heads, only to fail as new ones grew back. Finally, in a moment of inspiration, Hercules realized that strength alone would not defeat the monster. He needed ingenuity. After decapitating one of the hideous heads, Hercules would use fire to burn the wound shut, thus preventing a new head from growing. Using this method, the hero eventually defeated the Hydra and went on to face several more challenges.

At our institutional research office, we realized that faculty data had many "heads," each representing a different source of data. The heads were made hideous by the fact that one data source would not match another. For example, the vice president–chief academic unit offices and the human resource offices would both maintain data on faculty ranks, address, salary, and demographics. However, ask the departments for average faculty salary by rank and gender, and two "heads" would come up, snapping and snarling, each insisting that its information was correct. Once we resolved the issue, effectively cutting off the heads, a new source would emerge, in this case the provost's office. The provost's faculty data would again diverge from the previous two, and the office would also insist that its information was correct. Meanwhile, the same battle would be waged with data on grants, formal instructional activity, and student thesis and dissertation supervision. Faculty data were kept in various forms (for example, paper, spreadsheets, databases, and Web pages) in various offices (for example, Sponsored Research, Graduate College, Industrial Liaison, Human Resources, and vice-president offices) or with various individuals (the faculty themselves) who had little contact with one another concerning the data. We needed to use our ingenuity.

Based on our analysis, we identified several weaknesses in faculty data storage and utilization that could be addressed by developing a central faculty database:

• Similar faculty information was stored in a number of offices. There was a need to establish a central site for data and areas of responsibility, with one unit having domain over each specific portion of faculty data. Other departments would then use this source, effectively eliminating the duplication of effort. Individuals could also use this central source to search for information about all faculty, all computer science faculty, or all faculty working with waste disposal treatments.

• Information was stored in a variety of formats, making retrieval difficult. A number of departments were tracking salaries, demographics, and other attributes electronically, which made data retrieval manageable. But other qualitative information, such as publications lists, was kept in a paper-and-pencil format that was difficult to use at the aggregate level.

• Little intracampus data sharing took place. This produced duplication of effort and inconsistent information.

• The annual faculty evaluation form, called the Faculty Activity Report (FAR), a rich source of information about faculty, was kept in a paper-and-pencil format. Faculty completed the FAR annually as part of their performance review, after which it was filed away, never again to see the light of day. OIIR could not fulfill requests that required aggregate FAR information because we would have to examine each faculty paper report individually.

• FAR information sections were not clearly categorized. For example, in the "publications" section, one could not easily tell whether a given citation was a journal article or a book chapter. The sections provided a simple organizational structure that served the report's evaluative nature but were not useful for aggregate analysis.

The nature of the faculty data made the data unreliable for standard reporting purposes and almost unusable for a variety of additional purposes. For example, a number of departments requested faculty information for nonappraisal purposes. The vice president–chief academic officer also wanted to showcase faculty strengths through a campuswide faculty report. Faculty productivity, in terms of research and publications, could be a major selling point used to attract students, industry, and research to IIT. In short, faculty information could be a marketing tool, and the vice president needed reliable data and means to quickly generate reports. The vice president realized, as Jones (1994) noted, that the institution lacked the data resources necessary to respond to emerging information needs regarding faculty, one of the institution's key assets. In addition, during our accreditation process, the North Central Association of Colleges and Secondary Schools (NCA) requested information on faculty contributions to the communities surrounding IIT. These requests could not be filled using the existing structure of faculty data.

Clearly, IIT needed a better means of storing and retrieving faculty information. We planned to centralize faculty data into one database and establish data domains and checking procedures. We also planned to streamline data collection and access by developing a Faculty Activity Report World Wide Web interface for the database that would allow faculty easy access to add and review their own data. The two-year project, known as the Faculty Database/Faculty Information Sheet (FIS), introduced a new responsibility to OIIR, one that was to prove more difficult than any database construction or Web development: system management.

The Technology: FIS Version 1.0. Having identified a need for a new approach to faculty data management, in the fall of 1996 OIIR established a steering committee of key administrators who used faculty data to plan a database and Web solution, review technical standards, and develop the database dictionary. We chose to focus initially on full-time faculty and to expand the database later to include part-time faculty.

Even though the FIS was not a new procedure for faculty but merely an electronic version of an existing faculty requirement, the committee felt that senior-level support was crucial to the success of this project to encourage faculty to participate. We also needed to communicate clearly the benefits of the FIS to faculty. We emphasized that the new process would allow us to showcase faculty strengths to potential students, industry and research partners, and other institutions worldwide, a benefit over the existing paper-and-pencil process. In addition, we planned end-user tools that would allow faculty to use their information for other purposes.

After the completion of the database dictionary, we created the Faculty Database (FDB) with information coming from two sources: faculty, through a Web-based front end, and downloads from various departments housing other databases (such as the grant information housed in the Sponsored Research database). The database was constructed using Microsoft Access 7.0. Both the database and the Web entry forms would be housed on a Dell PowerEdge 2100/200 server running NTServer 4.0. Internet Information Server 2.0 (IIS) was running on the server at the time, but we did not initially use this software. Instead, we designed the Web-based forms using Web Form Express (WFE), a shareware designed by Chris Walker.

WFE was a Structured Query Language (SQL)–driven software that used open database connectivity (ODBC) drivers to access and query Access databases. WFE offered ease of use and a simple but effective security system; in addition, it was inexpensive at $100. WFE would dynamically create Web pages based on a query that the Web designer wrote, allowing end users to insert new records and update or delete existing records. However, since WFE creates the Web pages from predefined templates, the designer has no control over the final look of a site. The dynamic pages WFE created were not suited to our needs, in that we wanted the Web pages to mimic the paper FAR. Therefore, we used WFE to drive our Web pages, but we designed the interface in-house using HTML.

Our goal was to mimic the FAR as much as possible; however our analysis of the FAR revealed that some basic categories of information were being requested in multiple places. For example, faculty were asked to provide institutional committee membership in one section and noninstitutional committee membership in another. We decided to merge similar categories into one category and give that one category various types. So, using the example just cited, we created a group called committees, and within this group we had institutional and noninstitutional types. In addition, for some existing categories, such as publications, we created types (journals, chapters, books, and so on). We did this to extract specific information from the database more easily.

Pilot testing with faculty and staff led to several enhancements:

- We provided additional training for faculty on using the FIS.
- We included and trained the academic unit support staff in FIS data entry.
- We developed an on-line guide to the system.

We rolled out the FIS Version 1.0 in the spring of 1997. Faculty responses were mixed, and although several faculty embraced the effort, the limitations of the software were hard to ignore. The WFE process took too long, and the interface did not look enough like the original FAR. Moreover, some faculty were comfortable with their old paper-and-pencil system and were reluctant to let go.

It also became evident during this inaugural phase that OIIR was undertaking a new role, one that we did not particularly relish at the time. We had become system administrators, overseeing the design and implementation of information systems. We now donned several new hats, such as system designer, technical support, system trainer, database manager, and system policymaker. Although OIIR deferred policy decisions on such things as citation format to the academic unit heads, we specified policies on data entry, information review, and report access and generation. We were going beyond providing just data and analysis to determining how best to retrieve and store data and then designing the necessary applications. In retrospect, if we had had a more proactive Computer and Network Services department then, as we do now, we would probably not have taken this step alone. However, as we will discuss later, we do not regret the path we are on now. This truly was the road less traveled, and it has made all the difference.

The Technology Revisited: FIS Version 2.0. Seeing that WFE lacked the robustness we needed for the FIS and that the first incarnation of the on-line FAR was not completely accepted by faculty, we decided to redesign the process from scratch. Our goal was to make the FIS user-friendlier. To try to ensure that the redesign would satisfy the end users, faculty were fully engaged in the redesign process. Faculty input was obtained via meetings with all involved academic departments, individual meetings with faculty, and more testing.

The database interfaces were completely redesigned and rebuilt from scratch in-house over the course of six months by a full-time staff member and a computer science student employed full time over the summer. The database was also expanded to include additional variables from the original database dictionary that had not been included on the traditional FAR, such as interest in talking with media about research. The FIS was redesigned to mimic the paper FAR completely while still maintaining category types, again to ensure that information could be retrieved easily. The FIS was written in HTML and JAVA Script, using the file formats of the Internet Information Server (IIS). IIS allowed us to create templates of our own for the various sections of the FIS, thus improving our Web maintenance abilities. In all, over fifteen thousand lines of code needed to be written, tested, debugged, and published.

During the redesign, we also completed the distribution of data domains, or areas of responsibility, to various nonacademic departments. Data domain implies that only one area owns or is responsible for one type of information. Changes to nondomain sources could not occur until the original source, the domain source, was updated. An example will help illustrate why this was important. Human Resources (HR) maintained addresses for all personnel at IIT, and OIIR extracted address information from HR and uploaded it to the Faculty Database. However, although OIIR (nondomain) now had the address information, the integrity of the data were still HR's responsibility—HR had domain over address data. Any address change in the Faculty Database needed to be confirmed by HR and changed first in the HR system, after which it could be officially changed in the Faculty Database. Without this process, we would again have duplication of effort and inconsistent data. As part of this distribution of data ownership, interfaces were developed to facilitate data entry by several key staff. Data transfer relationships were also established between the database and the HR system, Sponsored Research, the Graduate College, and the vice-president–chief academic officer.

We rolled out the beta version of FIS Version 2.0 in the fall of 1997 for an extended four-month trial period, allowing faculty to use the database in order to identify any remaining bugs in the programming. Faculty came back with a number of suggestions for improvement, but the comments were more encouraging than those from the first version. From the spring to the fall of 1998, we enhanced the FIS and FDB and attempted to eliminate all kinks and bugs. Unfortunately, we also lost the student programmer, who had done the majority of the code for the second version of FIS. It took us months to find a suitable replacement, and this dramatically slowed the time frame of this project. By late 1998, the database was ready for permanent release, scheduled for spring 1999. Readers can view the FIS by going to oiir.iit.edu and then choosing IIT Faculty and then the Faculty Information Sheets (FIS) and Faculty Activity Reports (FAR) link. Click "Continue" and use the following "dummy" logon: user name, *rishi*; password, *blitzen*.

Implications for IR. The trials and tribulations of the FIS illustrate how technology has changed the role of one IR office. It is often thought and perhaps even true that technology enables us to be more efficient data collectors, speedier data analyzers, and more robust data disseminators, allowing information to be sent virtually anywhere in a number of electronic formats. However, technology has also propelled us into areas once reserved for staff in central systems and computer programmers. Inexpensive and relatively easy-to-use software, combined with more powerful desktop computers, allow researchers to manage information in ways that in the past were often too time-consuming or too difficult for a small office such as ours.

All is not golden, however, in this new age of technology. The new role of systems administrator brings with it a variety of new responsibilities, costs, and trade-offs. Technical support and database management are just two of the new tasks the institutional researcher must face. These new tasks question the staffing and typical structure of the IR office and the allocation of resources.

As a result, in many of today's institutional research offices, personnel are no longer just researchers; they are also technical experts. For example, at IIT, the data analyst position in OIIR was recently reclassified to an information manager position, adding a number of technical responsibilities not previously included in the data analyst job description. In addition, we now require additional technical support, much of which we draw from the talented and hardworking student employees our office has been very fortunate to employ. A few years ago, we employed students to enter data and stuff envelops for survey mailings; today our students design databases and Web-based front ends for complex databases.

An outgrowth of these changes for OIIR has been the clear and conscious bifurcation of staff knowledge, skills, and abilities, which drives our dual-track office agenda of research and information technology. Changes in technology have allowed us to explore new activities, sometimes at the expense of more traditional IR projects. When the IR office goes beyond drawing data from institutional information systems into the mechanics of developing new systems of gathering and storing information, even with faster software for data analysis and dissemination, time saved is not time earned. It is time reclassified.

Back to the central theme of this chapter: did the FIS make storing and retrieving faculty data faster, cheaper, and better? The answer to all three is yes and no. We have already used the FDB to compile information for a number of requests. We have satisfied not only the usual salary and demographic requests but nontraditional requests for publications and professional activities as well. For any of these requests, we were able to write queries—sometimes in minutes, sometimes taking a few hours—to extract the data. The information was then instantly displayed on our desktop monitors, which we could then cut into documents or print for further use.

Compared to the earlier case with the NCA in which we could not extract any information about faculty activities, the new process is much faster. However, we need to factor in time spent constructing and maintaining these data sources. The FIS has been a time-consuming process for the past two and a half years, occupying much of the part-time programmer's position and about 15 percent of one full-time position. More work still needs to be done.

This project also came with a price tag. We had to buy a new server, pay for the initial software, and compensate our student programmer and the full-time employee. The system will require continual maintenance. The technical skills that are necessary for the job ensure that the full-time staff and student workers who supply the technical know-how will be compensated at rates higher than average. However, when we can produce reports from the database at a faster rate, we do not waste people-hours (which translate into dollars) trying to track down various pieces of information.

Are the data better? The most important and beneficial aspect of this entire experience is that the quality of the previously stored non-FAR data (such as demographics, addresses, and faculty attributes) has improved. With the establishment of data domains, we have reduced redundancy and ensured that the parties who are most vested in the data now oversee its integrity. We will be able to report and soon conduct research using faculty data with more accuracy and greater confidence.

However, quality control is not necessarily the product of technology but rather can be enabled by it. Data quality is an ongoing struggle in IR offices, with or without technology. Technology just makes this job a little bit easier, by simplifying and automating tasks. Using the paper Faculty Activity Report as an example, it was unfathomable to think about collecting, organizing, and cleaning the data on these paper reports. When we created a database for the information and a Web front end for faculty, the process was simplified and the maintenance was automated.

Are the FAR data in the FIS of better quality than the paper versions of the FAR? No. In either version, the data entry of information, dates, references, or activities may be inaccurate. Is the data processing better? Resoundingly yes. Ultimately, IR will need to draw from both new technology and traditional IR skills to provide high-quality and meaningful data and analysis—the real name of the game.

Case Study 2: Willamette University—Turning a One-Person Shop into a Web-Based Enterprise

Willamette University (WU) is a liberal arts university in the Pacific Northwest with nearly 2,500 students, most of whom attend full-time. Founded in 1842 by Methodist missionaries, WU consists of the very traditional undergraduate College of Liberal Arts, the College of Law, the School of Education, and the Atkinson Graduate School of Management.

The office of Institutional Research and Planning Support (IRAPS) at Willamette University began loosely in November 1994 with the creation of a formal institutional research function. The office became an independent department of the university in the spring of 1996. It quickly became apparent that this one-person office with far too many requests to handle was in great need of technology-based solutions.

The three years following the creation of IRAPS have been extraordinarily dynamic:

- Willamette's president of seventeen years stepped down, followed by a one-year interim before a new president was chosen.
- Other senior administrators departed and were replaced.
- The administrative system was subject to a major upgrade.
- The information culture of the institution shifted to a more data-driven model.

These dynamics of change are not uncommon. The first case study recounted a period of organizational change at IIT that led to the IR office; other authors in this volume have noted that change is one of the most pervasive trends in higher education today. Many institutional research offices exist in very dynamic environments that in many ways may now be considered "business as usual." In any event, these dynamics create a challenging environment and tensions that are not easily ignored. For IRAPS, this meant an increased number of information requests.

Cycles in IRAPS. Technological advancement is an evolutionary process, whether in the world or within the confines of the institutional research office. The development of solutions to ease the burden of the institutional research office at Willamette University was evolutionary and tied to the cyclical nature of the IRAPS office.

Census Cycle. As noted, Willamette University has a strong college of liberal arts and professional programs in law, management, and teaching. Typically, 40 percent of the annual degree awards go to these professional students. Summer sessions are nearly nonexistent, and fall headcounts rarely exceed 2,500. These semesters form the primary cycle of census reports.

Willamette University reports census as of the tenth day of classes in the College of Liberal Arts (CLA), which corresponds to the end of the add-or-drop period. The Enrollment Reporting Series (ERS) collection of reports is approximately thirty-five pages long and is usually released within eight working days of the census. The three weeks from the start of the term to the publication of the ERS consume a lot of processing time in IRAPS for data verification and consultation with the university registrar, the Atkinson School registrar, and the College of Law recorder.

IPEDS Cycle. Overlapping this cycle are the compliance reports, or Integrated Postsecondary Education Data System (IPEDS) surveys. As with all other Title IV institutions, Willamette is mandated by law to complete these reports in order to maintain Title IV eligibility. The IPEDS cycle currently stretches from August through March.

Financial Aid Cycle. The third major cycle is the student recruiting and financial aid award cycle that begins the last week of March. At this time, IRAPS begins weekly publication of a thirty-eight-page report analyzing the current financial aid risk and reward scenario. As a highly selective liberal arts college, Willamette University awards an average of $10,000 to 85 percent of its incoming freshmen, with a potential risk of $10 million against a $3.2 million budget. This publication provides crucial information to the enrollment management team for decision making. This cycle lasts from the end of March through the fall census.

End-of-Term Cycle. The final cycle is the end-of-term reporting. This includes reports on such topics as rank in class, course summaries of student success and failure, and faculty teaching load.

These cycles inform and structure more than half of the annual functions of IRAPS. Ad hoc reports, committee work, long-term technical development projects, and targeted support projects must all be done during and around these cycles. Further, these operations must take place in a politically, technologically, and systemically dynamic environment.

Originally, IPEDS reports and other enrollment reports were very often prepared by simply counting and tallying lists of students from blue-bar computer printout. This was certainly not the most effective way to complete these tasks, particularly in 1994. The intent was to create an integrated solution that would provide a stable, flexible, and powerful platform for the future of institutional research at Willamette.

Database Technology. The technology of the IRAPS office, like that of IIT's Faculty Database project in the first case study, can be broken into two components: database technology and the Web. Though database technology is not as flashy as Web design or multimedia data modeling and perhaps does not inspire anything other than groans, new database design and development techniques have made ad hoc and standardized reporting and analysis much easier and adaptable to systemic changes.

IROQUOIS. From the beginning, the IR function at Willamette was established around a relational database concept known as IROQUOIS—the Institutional Research Office Quick Information System. This database was designed to support standard and ad hoc reporting with as much automation as possible. IROQUOIS is a collection of Microsoft Access databases representing nearly all the data operations and relations of the institutional research office. Viewed as a whole, IROQUOIS contains snapshot tables, valid value tables (code definitions), derived tables, templates, queries, reports, and code modules that support research and reporting. What sets IROQUOIS apart from the administrative system or other databases is that it is designed as an analytical database as opposed to a transactional database.

An administrative database, such as a student information system, is designed for entering and retrieving individual records or producing bulk reports in the form of class rosters, report cards, and billing statements. There may be dozens of summary reports and status reports, but those tend to be of little use to an institutional researcher. As Chan notes in Chapter One, an analytical database is designed not for record keeping but for analysis.

What does this mean in real terms? An analytical database possesses qualities that enhance analysis and allow for quick response:

- It allows for longitudinal or point-in-time analysis: the structure of the database should allow easy tracking of a cohort (or multiple cohorts) of students through successive academic terms or years.
- It allows for quick setup and rapid development of ad hoc queries.
- It is fully relational and supports referential integrity.
- It is not fully normalized: full normalization of the tables and database can slow down the process of query building and increase the user's knowledge requirement (which tables are related to which, what the proper field associations are, and so on), and transitional data can be lost.
- It includes support tables to create row headers and force fixed-format reporting: in normal database reporting, if there are no observations for a particular category, that category drops out; using this technique, the analyst can guarantee that the report format will always be the same.

Many experts will argue with some of these qualities, particularly the issue of normalization. However, this represents a trade-off of efficiencies that essentially boils down to convenience versus disk space. Disk space is increasingly cheap (and getting cheaper every day), and a person's time is a far more valuable resource. Perhaps violating a few theoretical principles is necessary to achieve an optimal design.

IROQUOIS was conceived as a seamless one-stop shop for data, once the data were extracted from the administrative system or acquired from other sources. To this end, it has served very well. After nearly four years, IROQUOIS has evolved into Version 2.0 to realign the data with changes in the administrative system that resulted from the conversion from Datatel

Rev. 13 to Rev. 14. This conversion was a major overhaul in many areas of the student system. Although the financial aid file structures were nearly untouched, the registrar modules were completely redesigned with new file names, field names, data relationships, and valid value code tables.

Rule-Based Processing. The most exciting evolution in the IROQUOIS database technology has been the movement to rule-based processing. Rule-based processing (RBP) is a derivation of the rule-processing routines found in business systems and administrative systems. The important difference between RBP and business rule processing is that the rules in this RBP system are used in report processing and analysis instead of live look-up procedures. For example, a business rule might read "if $x = y$ and $z = > 0$, then display a; else display b for k" in pseudocode (a mix of English language and programming code) and be executed anytime the value of k is requested. In RBP, the rule is broken into code fragments that are reassembled and executed only in the course of creating a static report.

In simple programming terms, RBP works like this: a target output is designed, and each line (or cell, if necessary) is related to a table of rules that defines the conditional values of an SQL statement. Once the rules are developed, an SQL statement is created within a code module in the body of a "do" loop. The function of the code module, or "rules processor," is to read the rules table and substitute the SQL conditional statements for placeholder variables in the SQL statement from the rules table. The SQL statement is then executed for each set of rules. The process is explained in the flowchart in Figure 3.1.

A simplified example will help clarify this in terms that even a novice programmer can understand. Start with a result table that lists categories of students down the left side and financial aid categories across the top, as in Table 3.1. The rules table would look like Table 3.2.

Keep in mind that this is a simple example and thus there is some redundancy in the cell definitions. The remaining piece to this example is a code module that reads the rules table one line at a time and plugs the values into an SQL statement that it then executes. The SQL statement would be similar to this:

```
"INSERT INTO OutputTable (Group, Column1, Column2, Column3) " &
GroupText & "' As GroupText', Sum(" & Column1Rule & ") As Col1, Sum("
& Column2Rule & ") As Col2, Sum(" & Column3Rule & ") As Col3 FROM
DataTable Where((" & GroupRule & ")) GROUP BY '" & GroupText & "';"
```

Note that the column headings from Table 3.2 are embedded in the SQL statements between double quotes and ampersands. This is Visual Basic for Applications (VBA) syntax for string concatenation. As the table values are read, they are substituted in the string to complete a properly formatted SQL statement. The resultant table might look something like Table 3.3.

An unplanned benefit of this evolution is that since output is now directed to a data table, Web publication is greatly simplified. Standard

Figure 3.1. RBP Programming

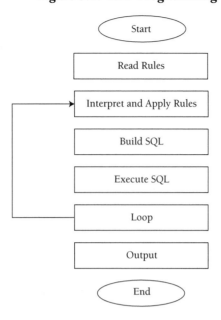

HTML template files can be created that access these tables with little effort. Furthermore, these summary tables can be exported or linked to any other desktop application for other forms of publication.

The greatest single benefit of RBP is that it is much easier to open a rules table and modify a set of rules to reflect changes in the administrative system than to go back and modify thousands of lines of code. For example, our standard enrollment reports (the ERS) were producible after the conversion to Datatel Rev. 14 with extraordinarily little work consisting of only modifying the various tables of rules. In fact, it was surprising how easy it was. Another powerful benefit of this process is its utility for projects other than analysis, such as data distribution and warehousing, including Web-based storage. These reports can be found on the Web at ir-server.willamette.edu/enrollment.

Web Technology. The second part of the IRAPS solution is Web technology. Whereas IRAPS used database technology primarily to streamline the ability to generate information related to the various reporting cycles and ad hoc information, Web technology made a wide variety of information more accessible to the user on a "need to know" basis. The ERS Web site allows users to focus easily on one school or group of students. Moreover, it allows term-to-term comparisons within each report. The Web has also been used for data collection in student surveys.

Paralleling the experience of many other institutional research offices, the initial steps in creating the IRAPS Web site were more of a stagger than

Table 3.1. Result Table

Group	Need-Based Institutional Aid	Merit-Based Institutional Aid	Non-Institutional Aid
New Freshmen #			
New Transfers #			
Total Undergraduate $			
New Graduates and Professionals #			
Total $			

Table 3.2. Rules Table

GroupText	GroupRule	Column1Rule	Column2Rule	Column3Rule
New Freshmen #	ForT='F' and StartTerm= CurrentTerm And Program='1'	IIF(Need> 0, 1, 0)	IIF(Nz(Need) =0, 1, 0)	IIF(Yearly_Aid > 0 And Yearly_WU=0, 1, 0)
New Transfers #	ForT='T' and StartTerm= CurrentTerm And Program='1'	IIF(Need> 0, 1, 0)	IIF(Nz(Need) =0, 1, 0)	IIF(Yearly_Aid > 0, 1, 0)
Total New Undergraduate $	StartTerm= CurrentTerm And Program='1'	IIF(Need>0, Yearly_WU, 0)	IIF(Nz(Need) =0, Yearly_WU, 0)	IIF(Yearly_Aid > 0 And Yearly_WU=0, Yearly_Aid, 0)
New Graduates and Professionals #	StartTerm= CurrentTerm And Program In '('2', '3', '4', '5')	IIF(Need> 0, 1, 0)	IIF(Nz(Need) =0, 1, 0)	IIF(Yearly_Aid > 0, 1, 0)
Total New Graduate and Professional $	StartTerm= CurrentTerm	IIF(Need>0, Yearly_WU, 0)	IIF(Nz(Need) =0, Yearly_WU, 0)	IIF (Yearly_Aid > 0 And Yearly_WU=0, Yearly_Aid, 0)

Table 3.3. Final Table Results

Group	Need-Based Institutional Aid	Merit-Based Institutional Aid	Non-Institutional Aid
New Freshmen #	45	30	25
New Transfers #	10	3	37
Total Undergraduate $	535,500	367,000	886,600
New Graduates and Professionals #	0	23	77
Total $	0	230,000	1,345,700

a series of leaps and bounds. The IRAPS office began with static graphic images of entire pages and then moved to HTML tables as the technology grew. Initially, database programming using rules tables to create hundreds of static pages in minutes created most of the Web site. Now the technology makes live database queries at a variety of levels a common feature.

For example, apart from the summary data contained in the ERS Web pages, the financial aid director has access to current lists of students selectable by major with data on need, institutional award, class standing, and start term. These data are updated daily. In the same protected directory, the financial aid director can access a report based on the admissions ranking and financial aid matrix for incoming freshmen and undergraduate transfers. This report is updated every two hours.

IRAPS Web Reports. IRAPS provides a wide range of information on the Web site, including basic policies and procedures information, snapshot and historical trend enrollment reports, and special studies reports.

• *Policies and procedures.* Textual data regarding policies, definitions, and procedures change relatively infrequently. These items exist in static HTML pages. Examples of these include the IRAPS office's Polices, Operations, and Procedures manual (including the AIR Code of Ethics) and the definitions associated with the ERS.

• *Term-based snapshot enrollment data.* Snapshot data, usually term-based, are accessible through a process of Web-based look-up. For example, a dean can evaluate enrollment trends in a course in a variety of ways, including drill-down focus by instructor, by going to the IRAPS Web page and "clicking" to the pages of information on enrollment trends. This type of information has been particularly popular with deans as a planning tool for resource allocations.

• *Term-based summary reports.* As mentioned earlier, one of the unintended benefits of RBP was the creation of summary tables within the database. These tables are automatically available in an information warehouse that allows users to look at a standard semester report or longitudinal report of their own selection. Once the ERS is complete, the summary tables are made available automatically in the database on the Web server, usually by the end of the third week of the semester.

• *Snapshot data.* IRAPS provides daily snapshots of data such as currently enrolled students by major and minor to provide users ready access to such information.

• *Historical enrollment data.* A ten-year history of course enrollment may seem rather "vanilla" compared to benchmarks and comparisons, but it is quite powerful as evidenced by a story related by an associate dean. When the associate dean suggested to a department chair that the enrollment in a specific course was rather small and another course should be offered in its place, the department chair claimed it was unusually underenrolled that semester. The associate dean then went to the Web site, looked up the history for that course, and called the department chair back to explain that the course in question had never had more than three or four students in it and that another course would seriously be considered in its place.

• *Special studies and reports.* This category includes such reports as a faculty teaching load study, the largest special report, that is locked away in a password-protected directory for the dean's use. This is another ten-year overview that examines the course load of each faculty member with summaries by department, course level, and discipline area. The dean can print these out for use by individual departments. Current plans call for the expansion of this information in order to provide individual access for all faculty to their own reports and departmental summaries.

Overall, providing these reports and information over the Web saves paper and processing time by allowing IRAPS automatically to update and make corrections in a more timely fashion than might otherwise be possible. Operationally, information requests can be rerouted to the Web, and users can get an immediate response, which is becoming more the exception than the rule for this one-person office. The biggest drawback is the additional responsibility for maintaining a server and the greater knowledge requirement that goes along with server configuration and maintenance.

Implications for IRAPS. As the role of IRAPS has evolved, so have the skills, knowledge, and abilities of the position of the director. The director is now a developer-programmer as much as a researcher, assuming a function that was at one time considered tangential to the position's responsibilities. This development echoes the first case study, where we noted the evolution of the research analyst position to that of technical information manager also because of attempts to embrace information technology solutions.

In addition to changing the nature of the director position, technology has changed the perception of information at Willamette. Administrators now think that information is easy to collect and readily available and that many of the IRAPS reports are "push-button reports." Consequently, administrators and executives have demanded more data.

These perceptions are, however, patently false. Although IRAPS has automated many reports and operations, the information undergoes a fair amount of review and analysis prior to its electronic publication. The myth seems to arise because of the lack of technological skills in other offices. IRAPS is able to extract data and do complex analysis in a much shorter time than other offices in part because the data have already been extracted from the administrative system. Offices that do all their work in Colleague (the Datatel student module), for example, have only minimal character-based tools available and struggle with a variety of conversion and extraction issues. Furthermore, the technical responsibilities of the director of this one-person shop account for a growing proportion of on-the-job time. For instance, the director must be able to provide technical as well as interpretive support for Web-based reports.

Nevertheless, technology has had its advantages. Report debugging is easier with the incorporation of RBP. It is also much easier to build and add warehousing features to the Web site. RBP also greatly enhances information delivery, in terms of both quality and quantity. In addition, Web delivery tools reduce paper use and provide almost instant feedback. Web server logs provide indicators of the demand for certain kinds of information and the frequency of system use.

Transformations: IR Skills for the Information Age

These two case studies provide a snapshot of the impact of technology on the IR office. The first case discussed the planned development of a database and Web interface to facilitate data collection and utilization. The second described how a small information office evolved to use database and Web tools to streamline information production and expand access to critical information. Both used database software and the networking capabilities of their institutions.

Consequently, both IR offices experienced significant changes and realignments in terms of staff skills, functions, and resources. In the case of IIT, substantial resources were allocated to the database project, in terms of both staff time and technical support. This project caused the office to rethink its structure and reorganize to prepare for new technological challenges. At Willamette University, the technical skills of the IR director evolved, and the perception of push-button reports created the illusion of speed that fueled the desire for more information.

Both cases show how the institutional researcher's role has changed. The IR professional and data user is now the information architect, designing and developing information systems that produce, house, and distribute information to users for decision making and planning. Out of this come a variety of new Web, database, and technical support skills necessary for IR that challenge us to rethink issues of organization and resource allocation.

Web Mastery. The growth of the Web as an information management tool has turned many institutional researchers into "Webmasters"—now an additional job function. These IR professionals have had to learn about controlling access to the site and server and shared database configuration, as well as less arcane skills such as advanced document-to-HTML conversion and site planning. Sometimes embracing the Web has occurred by choice, at other times out of sheer necessity to develop information-oriented solutions to address client needs. For example, the development and growth of the Web capacity at Willamette was a mixture of, on the one hand, initial reluctance followed by greater interest in Web publishing and, on the other, a driving need to make more data and information available to a greater number of clients without a matching increase in budget.

New Skills in Database Design and Programming. From both case studies, it should be apparent that the design of databases went far beyond that of simply designing snapshot tables and research files. Thoughts about relationships, normalization, and how the data would eventually be processed and accessed were incorporated early on. The application of RBP and Web technology to databases was a major advance in information technology requiring new skills.

The research analyst position at IIT grew into an information manager position. With this came new expectations, including

- The capability to execute projects using the best and most affordable technology available
- A traditional IR knowledge base (for example, university structures and statistical and report writing capabilities)
- Knowledge of information systems development, design, and management skills

To this end, at IIT we supplemented our own limited knowledge by drawing on the expertise of several computer science students. However, we have this luxury as a technical university.

At Willamette, the situation was substantially different. While limited support was willingly offered, it was based in Unix skills and a different model of access. As a longtime Microsoft developer, the director was able to bring a full set of IR skills and a full set of software development skills to the situation.

Technical Support. In both case studies, the IR offices had to rely on in-house skills and ingenuity to solve problems. At IIT, when OIIR was formed, the computer services department was involved primarily in maintaining the central systems and was without a clear customer-service focus in database and Web technologies. In short, it was every office for itself. IR forged ahead, supplementing its skill sets with student programmers, retraining sessions, Web resources, and (mostly) trial and error. Willamette went through a similar set of circumstances, learning as it went along and relying on support from outside the office to supplement in-house expertise.

Of even greater concern for the IR offices from the perspective of resource management was the necessity to provide support to its client base for the available projects. Even the easiest interface needed to be explained, and a certain amount of handholding was always necessary.

Implications for IR

Better, faster, cheaper? We started with this question, and at this point the reader is probably wondering if we have met these goals and what the trade-offs have been.

- *Better?* Without question, faculty and administrators at both institutions have better access to data and information, much of which serves various traditional IR functions. The data themselves are not necessarily better, however, since the integrity of the source data has not been improved.
- *Faster?* Technology allows us to provide users with information that is only a few mouse clicks away. They perceive this to be "faster," although

the behind-the-scenes technology often adds another layer of preparation, making the up-front work slower. However, with good design principles and practices, the up-front work does not slow or complicate the entire process.

• *Cheaper?* At this point, probably not. There are hard costs for servers, development tools, backup processes, and a variety of hardware and software requirements. In addition, there are a variety of soft costs that are often overlooked, including costs for training, system research, and testing—not to mention the hardest cost to quantify, trial-and-error learning.

In general, successfully implementing new technology solutions requires IR to make decisions about the impact of technology on the administrative culture. For example, getting information out quickly satisfies the user but also creates the perception that the IR office has extra time to produce more information. A well-executed process can be faster and can provide the clients with what they need before they even ask. At Willamette, the deft use of database technology and a strong Web design allows users to access new information in a matter of days or even minutes or hours. At IIT, data that could only have been mined slowly from paper sources in days if not weeks can now be viewed in a matter of minutes from the faculty database. However, this increase can add new burdens to an already taxed IR office, especially a one-person show, as is the case at Willamette.

In addition, technology solutions use office resources differently and may use all or more of the resources than were required to complete these tasks the old-fashioned way. From our experiences, streamlining office functions may create opportunities to reallocate resources to systems maintenance and training, both in the short term and over time.

In addition to these organizational culture issues, the growing arsenal of technical skills and abilities has implications for the future development of the professional:

• *Greater hybridization between researcher and technical developer*
  Broadened access to new professional markets outside of higher education
  Rising personnel costs (technologists can often demand higher salaries)
  New problems such as poor documentation standards and use of non-
     standard logic and design structures by practitioners without formal
     training as developers
  Unknown long-range effects of short-term solutions
• *Professional staffing costs*
  Difficulty in hiring and keeping "exotic" combinations of skills
  Difficulty keeping highly mobile professionals
  Redistribution of technology-oriented projects to nonresearchers, with
     concomitant problems of nonstandard work habits
  Possibility of creating team-based approaches to develop and provide
     high-tech information products (assuming the technology division is
     adequately staffed) across administrative units (we had the advantage
     of a technical background from the beginning of these projects,
     whereas most IR practitioners will need to seek out training—from

the AIR Information Technology Institute, for example—or develop relationships with campus technical staff)
- *Evolutionary job descriptions and office functions*
  Should IR be kept as the core, or should a new hybrid be created?
  Is this hybrid professional any different than the knowledge-worker concept found in today's technology journals?
  Does this represent a bastardization of the "true" IR function?
  What is the long-range impact on the institution's perceptions of IR's role? Will this lead to a demystification of the IR function or conversion of IR into a technician's role?
  Where does this new IR belong in the organizational structure of the institution?

Ideally, these last issues will be answered satisfactorily in the near future, because they represent the next stage of our professional evolution.

We hope that this chapter has provided some insight into the practical experiences of two offices in their efforts to implement technology solutions and an appreciation for the resulting rewards and challenges for the new IR office.

Reference

Jones, D. P. "Information for Strategic Planning: The Faculty Database." In J. F. Wergin (ed.), *Analyzing Faculty Workload.* New Directions for Institutional Research, no. 83. San Francisco: Jossey-Bass, 1994.

ED SCHAEFER is the information manager and research analyst for the Office of Information and Institutional Research at Illinois Institute of Technology and can be reached via e-mail at schaefer@iit.edu or on the Web at oiir.iit.edu.

TOD MASSA is the director of institutional research and planning support at Willamette University and can be reached via e-mail at tmassa@willamette.edu or on the Web at ir-server.willamette.edu.

4

*The author discusses how technology's impact on learning
and pedagogy—distance learning—presents new challenges to the institutional researcher.*

The Impact of Distance Education
on Institutional Research

Trudy Bers

Why is distance education the focus of an article in a *New Directions* issue
devoted to technology and institutional research? Why, anyway, should
institutional researchers pay attention to distance education? The answer is
simple: distance education is radically changing higher education.

An explosion is taking place in the number of distance education delivery agents and students enrolled in courses. Dolence (1998) notes the following statistics:

- Forty of the fifty states have adopted virtual university strategies.
- More than sixteen thousand courses are indexed on the World Wide Web.
- There are already over one million on-line learners.
- More than 350 companies produce courseware.
- More than one thousand corporations sponsor corporate universities.
- Commercial learning centers are proliferating and successful.

Dolence's examples reflect distance education delivered primarily via technology in an asynchronous format, clearly the arena in which the most dramatic, exponential growth is occurring. However, distance education actually
takes many forms, including old-fashioned correspondence courses; courses
delivered via audiotapes or videotapes; interactive television courses requiring real-time, location-specific participation; and on-line courses delivered
asynchronously through the Web. The newer forms of distance education
simply could not exist were it not for technology.

Distance education is related to other changes occurring in higher education as well, such as movements toward competency-based education,

credit for alternative learning experiences, and credentialing through industry or corporate mechanisms rather than through formal college degrees. Distance education facilitates and complements these other changes, delivering learning opportunities in nontraditional ways in nontraditional settings, often to nontraditional students.

I am convinced that distance education will have profound effects on the roles, necessary skills, relationships, and ways of doing business for institutional researchers. In this chapter, I explore what these effects may be. Specifically, I describe ways in which distance education is beginning to influence the current and emerging environment for conducting research about institutions, assessment, and strategic planning. Challenges brought forth by distance education are identified throughout. Next, I present results of a brief survey of institutional researchers in two- and four-year colleges regarding the ways in which they are responding to research demands driven by distance education. I conclude with some broad-based issues raised by distance education and some suggestions for how institutional researchers might address this new educational reality.

Change

Technology is an agent of change, both directly as it affects the ways in which people do their work and indirectly as it influences relationships and expectations. As Bolman and Deal (1991) note, change affects many aspects of an organization, including roles, necessary skills, power relationships, and existing agreements and pacts. Though distance education is not necessarily based on technology—consider old-fashioned correspondence courses, for example—the reality is that the explosion of distance education is due primarily to technology: interactive television courses, on-line courses delivered asynchronously via the Web, and courses available on CD-ROM. Such courses are dramatically affecting the organization, availability, traditional roles, nature of educational providers, delivery systems, and even the definition of what constitutes a "course." Taken one step further, distance education will inevitably change the way we think about higher education, because traditional definitions will apply only to a shrinking segment of the industry.

Though not directly caused by distance education, other changes emerging in higher education are often linked with it. Such changes include competency-based education, credit for alternative learning experiences, and credentialing through industry or corporate mechanisms rather than through formal college degrees. For simplicity, I include these related changes under the umbrella of "distance education."

To illustrate the importance of these changes, consider two candidates for a job to maintain and support an Oracle database at your institution. One has just earned a bachelor's degree in computer science; he has little work experience, though he claims to be familiar with Oracle databases. The other has passed the Oracle Certified Database Administrator test and has two years of work experience in an environment similar to yours; she has the equivalent of only one year of undergraduate work. Which person is more likely to be hired? (For a brief description of the Certified Oracle Database Administrator certification program and test, see Couchman, 1998. Other software companies, including Microsoft and Novell, have similar programs. These certification programs do not require formal study for individuals seeking certification; instead they focus on demonstrated competencies.)

Though it seems self-evident that distance education will affect institutional research, the extent to which the research community or key decision makers have thought about these effects is unclear. In 1997, the National Postsecondary Education Cooperative (NPEC)[1] convened a panel of experts to explore the impact of technology on data systems.

Though not charged to look at distance education per se, many panelists' comments and the papers written afterward tended to define *technology* operationally as "distance education." Because so much reporting of student enrollments, student outcomes, institutional characteristics, and revenues and expenses is in the domain of institution research offices and also because distance education is virtually a creature of technology, the issues identified by the panelists illustrate ways in which technology affects institutional research.

Cartwright (1998) identified six major, albeit overlapping, themes that emerged from the NPEC panel.

1. Growth in distance and technology-based education render traditional definitions of *student, faculty load, cost,* and other measures either meaningless or misleading.

2. Unbundling of educational services, such as curriculum development, course delivery, advising, and assessment, along with changing patterns of student attendance (multiple institutions, stop-in/stop-out), make it difficult to evaluate outcomes. A shift to learner-centered rather than institutionally centered data will further affect the utility and appropriateness of institutional research.

3. Faculty roles, including the definitions of workload and contact hours, are changing rapidly, but metrics for calculating and reporting these have not kept pace with these changes. Even more to the point, policies and practices associated with contracts, compensation, evaluation, and tenure have rarely been adapted or made sufficiently flexible to accommodate emerging faculty roles. Though not examined specifically by the NPEC panel, it should be noted that faculty involvement in activities such as advising is likely to change. For example, will advisers be expected to help students choose courses from a number of distance education providers to ensure that the courses are not duplicative and, in combination, satisfy degree requirements or otherwise meet students' objectives?

4. Student participation patterns, such as attendance at multiple institutions simultaneously, taking courses through nontraditional education providers (for example, proprietary schools and corporate-based training

sites), multiple transfers, and time away from school make it difficult to track students or to assess their educational outcomes. It is even difficult to report such basic indicators as completion or transfer.

5. New instructional delivery models will make it more difficult to evaluate student progress through postsecondary education and to assess their learning gains—cognitive or achievement measures attributable to enrollment in college courses. Competency-based measures are likely to grow in acceptability and feasibility, supplanting more traditional measures of seat time and credits earned. These new models relate as well to changing patterns of teaching and learning. There is growing emphasis on learner-centered instruction and lifelong learning for continual skill upgrading, professional development, and personal enrichment. Students taking courses for these reasons are less likely to want formal college credits than individuals seeking actual degrees.

6. The final theme of the panel was impact on Interdisciplinary Postsecondary Education Data System (IPEDS) financial reporting: whether and to what extent IPEDS can accommodate and accurately portray revenue streams and expenditures associated with distance education.

In the next sections, I have chosen to focus on the impact of distance education in three primary areas germane to institutional researchers and often assigned wholly or in part to their offices: research about institutions, assessment, and strategic planning.

Impact of Distance Education on Research About Institutions

Institutional research often depends on data and information that are defined, entered, designed, and reported by a variety of other offices in the college or university, as well as by external organizations such as state governing or coordinating boards or other educational institutions. Distance education is putting new pressures on these critical aspects of research and adding complexities to them. Failure to make appropriate adjustments and to accommodate distance education issues in existing data definitions, compilations, management, and exchanges will seriously erode the validity, comprehensiveness, and utility of many institutional research projects.

Data Definitions and Calculating Variables. A major impact of distance education is that it forces the reconceptualization of data definitions and calculations for many variables that are part and parcel of routine reports and analyses conducted by institutional researchers. To illustrate, think of three "standard" measures: faculty load, student population, and credit hours.

Faculty Load. Faculty teaching distance education courses may no longer have the sole responsibility for creating instructional materials, delivering lectures, organizing and facilitating learning activities, and evaluating student performance. Individuals with specific skills, such as developing courseware, might be assigned that role, while other faculty members might provide the courseware content. External certification examinations prepared by industry representatives or testing agencies could well supplant traditional instructor-developed-and-graded examinations.

Several years ago, Armajani, Heydinger, and Hutchinson (1994) proposed a new model for higher education. The "Educational Enterprise" paradigm they conceived unbundles educational services and contracts to provide them through four separate organizations, each of which specializes in a particular area: teaching, facilities, learning resources, and learning technology. Faculty would be part of the teaching organizations, which would provide instruction under contract to the Educational Enterprise.

The Educational Enterprise paradigm is not operational, though aspects of the University of Phoenix, Synergistics, and other agencies that package courses for delivery by instructors hired to implement the delivery but not to design and develop course contents come close. Nevertheless, the concept proposed by Armajani and his colleagues is intriguing for this chapter. The enterprise would foster new definitions of faculty roles by enabling faculty members to concentrate on the instructional services each was most interested in providing. The market-driven character of the enterprise means that either the market would sustain faculty members teaching in traditional ways or they would no longer have jobs. The entrepreneurial nature would also promote redefining faculty roles to improve cost efficiencies as well as quality of deliverables.

The National Center for Higher Education Management Systems (NCHEMS) has put forth the proposition that faculty are assets to an institution and that the nature and expectations for what these assets should be providing are changing (Jones, 1999). Jones suggests that the primary role of faculty is to deliver instruction. This delivery is distinguished by five activities that could be undertaken by different individuals who are responsible for designing the course or curriculum:

- Designing the course or curriculum
- Developing the course or curriculum through selection of materials and similar activities
- Delivering instruction through class meetings that cover previously selected material
- Mediating the learning process by helping students understand material
- Assessing individual student learning

Under the NCHEMS model, one could assign roles to different individuals, with the combination of their work incorporated into a single course.

An article in the *Chronicle of Higher Education* (Guernsey, 1998) provides another illustration of how faculty roles are changing. It describes the emergence of a new career track, that of "instructional designer." Former faculty members or individuals who had initially sought full-time teaching positions appear to be filling these positions, taking either primary or key support roles for preparing instructional materials that in the past faculty members were expected to produce by themselves. A key attribute of instructional designers is their expertise in both academic computing and college teaching.

This development is both practical and threatening. It is a natural extension and elevation of work done by audiovisual and academic technology support staff. Instructional designers provide valuable services for faculty who may feel overwhelmed by the demands of keeping up with their disciplines and becoming technologically savvy. At the same time, the more the work traditionally vested in faculty is outsourced, even to employees of the same institution, the less faculty might be perceived as pivotal to the institution, at least in terms of teaching. This has profound implications as well for faculty reward systems and criteria for tenure and promotion, particularly in institutions that give substantial weight to teaching.

Student Population. Distance education affects another variable typically used in institutional research, student population. No longer do courses begin and end during specific weeks of a semester. Rather, students may enroll continuously, often at more than one institution, so the course load of a single individual could vary by the week. Determining even the number of students enrolled at a single institution becomes problematic, unless the calculation is done at the end rather than near the beginning of an agreed-on period so as to include enrollments from courses that began at any point during the designated period.

This trend has led to some discussion about adding an annual unduplicated count of students to the IPEDS survey in addition to, or some might suggest in lieu of, the fall headcount now collected. No decisions have been made about this; such a change could certainly affect how and when institutions capture and tabulate data. Even if IPEDS continues to collect fall headcounts only, others interested in the number of students served by institutions will undoubtedly want to know the total number of individuals who take courses over the year. This change also has implications for schools with more transient or cyclical enrollments—for example, those with a significant number of individuals who enroll in winter, spring, or summer but are not included in the fall headcounts. Institutions themselves may benefit from having more complete counts of students, particularly if they want to report total number of individuals served.

Credit Hours. A final example of a commonly used variable requiring reconceptualization because of distance education is the credit hour, the currency on which college degrees are based, in that earning a degree depends solely on obtaining a specific number of credits in designated courses at a specified grade level. Implications of rethinking credit hours are challenging, complex, and intersect with other changes taking place in postsecondary education. A fuller discussion of some of the issues and implications is presented later in this chapter.

Sharing Data and Data Exchanges. Another area in which distance education affects institutional research derives from student mobility and enrollment in multiple institutions. This pattern has actually existed for years; Adelman (1998) found, for example, that 54 percent of students from the high school class of 1982 who had attended a four-year college by the age of thirty had actually enrolled in more than one school. The growth of distance education and the establishment of remote sites by colleges and universities are likely to swell the number of students who take courses from multiple institutions. A growing challenge will be to determine who these students are and how to count them, as well as how much duplication or overlap of services there might be as students avail themselves of assistance at more than one institution.

The institutional researcher who wants to portray his or her own institution can continue to rely on institutional databases. But to gain a greater understanding of what is really happening to students, it is essential to look beyond a single college or university, perhaps even beyond a single state's higher education system. For example, we can look at retention or completion within an institution, but from a national perspective and for a richer understanding of what is happening to people, it would be more informative to take a systems approach to retention and completion. What if an institution were to document that 20 percent of its freshmen left but transferred successfully and earned bachelor's degrees elsewhere? Would that not be an indicator of success for both the institution and those students? Such an approach demands both student-centered data collection and interpretation and a perspective extending beyond a single college or university.

The pressure to share data about students is already great; legislative and public tolerance for accepting answers such as "we don't know" when colleges are asked about the number of students who graduate or who transfer has been nearly exhausted. A 1995 survey conducted by the State Higher Education Executive Officers (SHEEO) revealed that thirty-two states had comprehensive databases at the state level, including both two-year and four-year public institutions. An additional nine states had some level of statewide or significant systemwide databases (Russell, 1995).

Independent institutions are more resistant to sharing, but their ability to hold out is likely to erode as legislators call for an accounting of the extent to which distance education, which so far carries a far greater expense than is usually realized, is really leading to greater productivity and efficiency. Most interpretations of the Family Education Rights and Privacy Act (FERPA) continue to shield independent institutions from being required to share or exchange unit record data. Although there is resistance to sharing, there is also competitive pressure to deliver services students and other stakeholders expect and demand. In their quest to understand the full extent and impact of distance education, private institutions will feel ever-growing obligations to share data.

Revamping Databases and Transcripts. Ewell (1998) suggests both to facilitate transfer and to represent students' learning outcomes more comprehensively, transcripts and databases will have to be remodeled. The student rather than the institution will need to become the principal unit of analysis, and learning experiences beyond traditional credit courses will need to be included. The key point is that as distance education evolves and related changes such as competency-based verification of learning expand, confusion about what constitutes a "credit" will grow. Student mobility across institutions will further exacerbate the confusion unless institutions are willing to accept transfer credits earned through nontraditional means at another college or university.

Currently, transcripts focus on courses taken, credits earned, and degrees awarded. Most transcripts provide detail only for courses taken at the institution issuing the transcript, so that a full history of a students' postsecondary education requires examining transcripts from all institutions attended. Courses are equated to traditional semester or quarter credit hours.

Contact hours are the commonly used metric for determining the number of credits associated with each course and ultimately the earning of a degree. For example, fifteen to sixteen hours of lecture usually translate into one semester credit. However, most distance learning, particularly when delivered asynchronously, is self-paced, not tied to a given number of minutes or hours in class. When distance education courses are, in content, nature of assignments, and expected student outcomes, structured to be comparable to traditional on-campus courses, the number of credits attached to the distance education course is rarely in question.

Packer (1998) has proposed the creation of "career transcripts," which combine features of academic transcripts and résumés. A career transcript will incorporate records of college courses and degrees, competencies documented through vehicles such as industry or corporate certification processes, and educational or workplace experiences and honors that indicate achievement or demonstrated abilities. The career transcript recognizes and emphasizes lifelong learning and the expansion of education across space and time.

For institutional researchers, replacing traditional transcripts with career transcripts will require dramatic revisions in conceptualizing and then calculating measures of student progress and institutional effectiveness. Who will lead efforts to create career transcripts or similar records is unclear. This may be an area where entrepreneurs both inside and outside the academy take the lead—for example, education administrators who see career transcripts as vehicles for generating fees for services and initiating novel ancillary services for students, or external businesspeople knowledgeable about formal colleges and universities but operating outside them who see this as a business opportunity.

The Relevance of Indicators of Quality. Although accrediting and accountability agencies of all sorts now stress outcomes more than inputs as indicators of quality, input variables are still used in a variety of national surveys and institutional promotions to illustrate the quality of a college. A recent special report prepared by the Institute for Higher Education Policy (1999) notes that distance education has the potential for undermining these traditional indicators of quality. Books in the library, faculty-to-student ratios, and other input measures, which continue to be used as indicators of quality, are quite irrelevant in the context of distance education.

The Separation of Policy and Practice for Distance Education from IR. The design and implementation of distance education programs, courses, and services may be handled at institutions by individuals who are not accustomed to thinking about data collection and reporting. Typically, these people are unaware of nuances or issues for research and reporting. Thus it is important for institutional researchers to be closely linked with the individuals making both policy-level and operational decisions about distance education. Determining whether this is taking place is problematic, however, since it appears that many institutions are pushing to implement at least some distance education to meet governing board or other external funding incentives. Institutions no doubt feel pressures to be "on the cutting edge" without having the time or foresight to think through the implications of their actions. Conversations I have had with administrators at other institutions about subjects such as the contractual implications of distance education and handling services for distance education students suggest that many issues are addressed only when actual questions or problems arise.

Impact of Distance Education on Assessment

Distance education fosters a number of challenges regarding the assessment of student learning outcomes, a central component of accreditation self-studies, accountability reports, performance funding systems, and other mandates for reporting and accountability. Because assessment is often a responsibility of the institutional research office, which may act, for example, as assessment coordinator or faculty consultant, it is important for institutional researchers to be aware of these challenges and strategies for addressing them.

Modes of Delivery. Ewell (1998) has noted three changes in the teaching-learning environment induced by distance education, each of which affects the assessment of student learning outcomes. The first change is pressures resulting from dispersed modes of instructional delivery; these in turn increase the difficulty of aligning instruction with originally established learning goals and maintaining standards. Moreover, distance education may affect learning in ways that are not yet understood or measured.

The second change results from pressures created by increasingly asynchronous delivery modes. Because students progress at different paces, monitoring and measuring their progress must be detached from traditional time-based practices and data systems built on units of time such as contact hours and semesters. Though perhaps not directly germane to institutional researchers, asynchronous delivery and decoupling courses from usual metrics such as meeting hours or weeks in a semester raise questions about faculty office hours, when best to provide advising, and how long a student should be considered to be "enrolled" in a course and eligible for the institution's support services even if apparently making no progress toward completion.

The third change suggested by Ewell is pressures arising from multi-institutional modes of instruction delivery. Student mobility across institutions, complicated by their earning competency-based certifications through nontraditional means, raises real questions about the extent to which a single institution can assess learning outcomes achieved at that college or even keep track of "credits" and "competency verifications" acquired elsewhere.

Related to this is the issue of college transcripts. As noted, the medium of exchange for transfer, the earned credit recorded on institutionally based transcripts, is no longer applicable in a distance education setting. The typical college transcript records grades and credits earned at the institution and the total of credits transferred to that institution from elsewhere or awarded through alternative means such as proficiency credit or portfolio analysis. Institutional transcripts might not, however, list the specific courses or course equivalencies of transfer or alternative credits and are even less likely to include information about noncredit learning experiences or external certifications. Unfortunately, this is the major resource used by institutional researchers to assess student progress and to calculate accepted, if not appropriate, indicators of institutional effectiveness such as graduation and transfer rates.

Academic Integrity. Distance education poses other assessment challenges as well. Many faculty remain skeptical about whether students in distance education classes are actually doing the work they submit. Though concerns about academic integrity are not a monopoly of distance education, they take on new dimensions in environments where instructors might never meet their students face to face, see examples of their handwriting, or hear their voices. In addition, faculty do not have the capability of giving in-person, real-time assignments that provide benchmarks about students' knowledge and abilities against which to measure out-of-class work and thereby to verify that the work really was done by the student.

Works in Progress. Time and permanency are another set of assessment issues. Web-based assessment submissions such as papers or projects, whether for course, programmatic, or institution-level assessment, can be modified continually by students. Unless the person collecting materials prints or saves the work at a specific point in time, it is never clear when the material is "final." This is analogous to the challenge of doing research on live rather than frozen databases. The former may be more current, but continual changes in the database make it virtually impossible to conduct research because one cannot return to the data source with confidence that it is the same each time.

Style Versus Substance. Another issue related to assessment is disentangling presentation from substance. McLean (1999) notes that skills and creativity are unevenly distributed in classes. Recall that students who take courses via the Web and who submit their papers via the Web have all the stylistic resources of the Web at their disposal. Some students are much more capable or interested than others in accessing these resources to enhance their Web-based assignments, using features such as background color and images, links, animation, and audio. This can be confusing and potentially misleading to the evaluator, who may inadvertently confuse style with content.

Complex linkages can pull the evaluator off track and make the flow of the "paper" difficult to follow. The use of nonstandard colors for links can also be problematic. McLean (1999) asserts that "when evaluating dozens of assignment products, the evaluator may come to depend upon the link colors as an indication of visited links (red means we have seen this one) and disoriented if the student elects to reverse the colors (so red means not visited)." But having visited a link, denoted through color, is not the same thing as reading, critiquing, and using information from that site in completing one's assignment. This is really no different from a student padding a bibliography, claiming to have consulted more references than he or she has, but evaluators will have to train themselves not to be seduced by color cues that come on Web-based assignments.

Reconceptualizing the Student Experience. Yet another assessment issue is reconceptualizing the student experience and then creating and administering assessment tools that are meaningful and appropriate to that experience. For example, it is normal to think of residential students as attending real-time, real-location courses, even if we acknowledge that some may supplement traditional classes with distance education classes. But there is a more dramatic pattern that can emerge: students living on campus because they want to be away from home and have the experience of campus life but taking all of their classes through distance education, never going to a classroom or interacting face to face with teachers or fellow students. How do we assess the experience and learning outcomes of these students? This scenario, suggested by Dan House, director of institutional research at Northern Illinois University, is but one illustration of the kinds of behavioral changes and attendance patterns that are likely to emerge as distance education becomes more ubiquitous and as students discover and create whole new ways to "attend" college.

Assessment of Learning in Traditional Classroom Settings. One of the unexpected consequences of distance education on assessment may be the challenge it poses for improved assessment of traditionally delivered education. Despite nearly a decade of accrediting agency demands for assessment and numerous state agency accountability mandates, institutions are still struggling with assessment. Skepticism about whether students learn through distance education and the need for distance education to "prove itself" may be prompting more thorough research about student learning outcomes in distance education than in traditional courses. But if a key criterion for demonstrating the value of distance education is that its students perform as well or better than on-campus students, then assessment of student outcomes in those on-campus courses and programs has to occur as well. A book by Thomas L. Russel (1999), *The No Significant Difference Phenomenon,* and a related Web site (teleeducation.nb.ca/nosignificantdifference) review over three hundred studies on the effectiveness of all types of distance systems. Russell concluded that there is no significant difference in learning outcomes when face-to-face and distance learning options are compared for the same populations.[2]

Some of the most interesting work about assessment and distance education is taking place in the competency-based curriculum at Western Governor's University (WGU), a virtual university. The competency-based credential delivered through WGU is premised on these fundamental assumptions: competencies are skills or knowledge identified by professionals in a particular field as being essential for mastery of that field; one can demonstrate competencies by completing assessments; and assessments take varied forms, including paper-and-pencil or computer-based tests or practical demonstrations of skills (Dolence, 1998). Instead of completing a set of courses to earn a degree or certificate, WGU students in the competency-based curriculum must demonstrate they have acquired a specific set of competencies. It may be that one of the most far-reaching effects of WGU will be advancing a national conversation about competency-based education and credentialing, regardless of setting.

Impact of Distance Education on Strategic Planning

A third major area in which distance education will affect institutional research is strategic planning. From a broad perspective, institutions may want to examine whether their use of distance education is truly promoting new ways of teaching and learning and of reengineering the institution. A narrower view would be to examine distance education as a new delivery mechanism premised on existing concepts of instruction (Privateer, 1999). The former is more frightening because it calls into question decades, if not centuries, of academic traditions. Therein lies the real challenge to strategic planning posed by distance education.

Regardless of which approach is taken, there are some key linkages that ought to be made, but rarely seem now to exist, between strategic planning and distance education. Indeed, it appears that in most institutions, planning for distance education is taking place as a separate process from more comprehensive or traditional planning.

Strategic Planning for Educational Delivery in an Integrated System. In most institutions, IR offices direct and manage or at least lend primary support to strategic planning efforts. Traditional strategic planning relies heavily on environmental scanning to detect external trends likely to have an impact on the institution, on competitive analyses to assess what other postsecondary institutions compete for and offer to the same pool of students, and on the identification of strengths, weaknesses, opportunities, and threats affecting the institution. Enrollment management, which is both strategic and tactical, will also be affected by distance education as opportunities for students to enroll in multiple institutions simultaneously or sequentially expand and as students opt to take certain courses through distance education from an institution other than their "primary" one.

In a recent Education Commission of the States policy paper, Mingle and Ruppert (1998) pose five issues regarding which states will have to play a leadership role. The issues exist at the institutional level as well and provide a framework for guiding strategic discussions about distance education and technology. The issues are state (or institutional) goals and priorities, statewide (or institutional) networks, new organizational structures, cost effectiveness, and financing and investment strategies.

Rapid Change. There are other factors to consider with respect to strategic planning. One of the most compelling is that changes are occurring so rapidly that it is difficult to project or imagine the future beyond two or three years. Thus time horizons for strategic planning need to be adjusted, and flexibility has to be a key element in both strategic planning processes and in plans themselves.

Growth of Alternative Providers. Another factor is the exponential growth in the number and variety of agents delivering postsecondary education and training, described earlier in this chapter. Identifying, understanding, and addressing "the competition" is growing more complicated, unpredictable, and frustrating. The environment in which a single institution or system operates is no longer constrained by geography, time, national borders, or definitions of entities that have the capability and authority to develop, deliver, and certify learning.

Assessing the Consequences of Entering or Not Entering the Distance Education Market. Institutions must decide whether and to what extent they will offer distance education and what the consequences might be if they choose not to. For example, will a college or university that does not offer any distance education be perceived as old-fashioned, unresponsive to customer demand, resistant to technology? How can distance education be effectively and efficiently integrated with other programs and services and be consistent with the institution's mission? Can the institution afford distance education? And how can the effectiveness and efficiency of its integration be measured?

Costs. Issues of cost are among the most important factors that need to be considered in strategic planning. Distance education has implications not just for resource use and allocations but for opportunity costs associated with investments in distance education. There are numerous generic and anecdotal assertions that technology will be a cost-effective approach to expanding the delivery of and access to education, enabling schools to do more with less. Privateer (1999) states:

> The literal presence of computers on campus, together with a decade-old call to "do more for less," factor heavily in the growing tendency of federal officials, governors, legislators, governing boards, and college and university administrators to envision instructional technologies as a panacea able to maintain the status quo while dramatically cutting delivery costs. The allure is certainly powerful: lower overall operating and administrative costs, more automated and time-independent instruction, less yet more "productive" instructors, greater course availability and offerings, and access to lower cost resource materials all translate into savings [p. 66].

Berge and Schrum (1998) suggest that a first step in assessing costs is to take an inventory of existing resources, including hardware, software, distance delivery technologies, and technical and faculty support staff, as well as to identify technology-enhanced projects already functioning. Armed with baseline data, financial analyses can then be made. Berge and Schrum assert that "technology-enhanced courses usually cost more to produce and deliver than traditional courses. . . . Once the analyses are made, the distance education program needs to be compared to other resource allocation opportunities that are presented to . . . the broader institutional decision-making structure for assessment and decisions on whether to move forward with the program and resource commitments" (p. 5).

Jewett (1999) has developed a simulation model, BRIDGE, designed to compare the costs of what they term "distributed instruction" (television or asynchronous network courses) versus traditional lecture or laboratory instruction. The model uses one hundred parameters, which can be modified by users to reflect their own situations or to engage in "what if" scenarios. Case studies testing the model provide findings about costs and benefits associated with various types of instructional delivery methods.

Yet another cost-related impact of distance education may result from students' choosing to take selected courses elsewhere. Although this has always been an option, the availability of distance education courses that a student can take from one college while enrolled primarily at or without even leaving another increases the potential for this to occur. Consider the fact that many institutions derive a disproportionate amount of their revenue from a small number of high-enrollment, low-cost general education and service courses offered at the lower division. What budget consequences will there be if students choose to take these courses through distance education from other providers, attracted by course attributes such as nationally known faculty, the entertainment value of instructional materials that capitalize on multimedia productions, and the desire to escape large lecture courses?

Integrating Planning Across Programs. Another effect of distance education on strategic planning is the need to integrate planning for distance education with planning for all academic programs. Organizationally, it is possible for distance education to be lodged in a separate department or college, much as continuing education is often separated from credit and degree programs. However, such segregation can exacerbate what some observers perceive as competition between traditional and distance education for resources and for students and promote the view that distance education is somehow not as legitimate or central to the institution as campus-based courses.

It is possible to conceive of a separate institutional research office for distance learning as well. Already some institutions have quite separate offices to conduct enrollment management studies and research assessing student learning outcomes. Fragmenting institutional research responsibilities across several offices that may not be in close contact can further complicate not just strategic planning but also the institution's decision-making processes and potential overlap, duplication, or wasting of resources.

Real Experiences, Challenges, and Possible Next Steps

The literature about distance education and its impact on institutional research or on data and information more generally is largely speculative, looking toward what should be happening or what might occur in the future. To glean a sense of what is really happening now, I conducted an informal survey of institutional researchers in my state, asking colleagues from both two-year and four-year institutions to respond to open-ended questions about how their institutions defined distance education, what impact distance education has had on their offices so far, and what they anticipate the future impact might be. Their responses provide some important glimpses into the "real world" of institutional research and its expectations regarding distance education.

My colleagues indicated that, at least in Illinois, the impact of distance education on institutional research is largely anticipatory. Most schools do not even have an agreed-on, operational definition of distance education. Only a handful of people have been involved in policy discussions, assessments, or considerations of data definitions and databases that can capture data and information about distance education. Some are beginning to track students, though not everyone has even coded courses to permit identifying students enrolled in distance education classes. Several respondents said they treat distance education students no differently from other students.

I asked about changes expected to occur, realistically, in the collection and reporting of data about students engaged in distance education over the next three to four years. Some of my respondents anticipated that more data about distance education students will be needed, but most either did not answer this question or said they don't expect distance education students to be differentiated from other students.

Conclusion and Next Steps

It appears that the impact of distance education on institutional researchers and their offices has not been meaningful in most institutions—yet. This generalization grows from a variety of indicators, including the informal survey I conducted, a review of the literature, conversations with individuals who are experts in distance education, and assertions of NPEC panelists. Speculations abound. The NPEC panel, for example, posed a number of questions and challenges (U.S. Department of Education, 1998). Though the panel used the term *technology,* it really dealt with distance education and technology-mediated instruction in the broadest sense. According to the panelists, these are the broad-based issues that will need to be addressed, many of which have been discussed in this chapter:

- Current surveys—for example, modifications in institutional and longitudinal surveys that will be required to capture changes in student behavior and participation
- New relationships between learners and providers—for example, definitions of program completers, new sponsors of learning, undermining the relevance of many traditional indicators of quality
- Using the student as the unit of analyses—for example, how we define students, how "completion" is determined, and how we can link students across multiple institutions, learning modes, and agencies that collect student-related data
- Student assessment in a technology-based environment

If we follow a more dramatic and extensive line of thinking, challenges will be even greater. Distance education could prompt the reexamination and possibly the reconceptualization of the ways in which instruction and the academic enterprise are perceived, organized, staffed, managed, physically located, funded, marketed, and evaluated.

Given this, what should institutional researchers do to prepare themselves and to be proactive in meeting research and data challenges of distance education?

- Think in new ways about what constitutes courses, credits, degrees, learning experiences, students, faculty, and institutions.
- Find and share concrete examples of what is actually being done in institutions that have some track record of distance education (this is not easy, since the literature is still replete with descriptions or speculations but contains few detail-oriented case studies or examples of problem solving).
- Look for opportunities to link with offices making policy and implementation decisions about distance education and the support systems under-

pinning not just distance education but also institutional databases, degree monitoring programs, and assessment of learning outcomes.

- Avoid being seduced by skepticism or the attitude that distance education is "just a phase" that will pass, leaving the traditional organization, structure, and delivery of higher education intact.
- Above all, look for opportunities to build bridges and create new partnerships and working arrangements. In the language of technology, enhance connectivity within and among institutions, because the most dramatic impact of technology and distance education is likely to be breaking down barriers—among postsecondary institutions; among roles of faculty and staff; among colleges and universities on the one hand and corporate or other education services providers on the other; among on-campus and off-campus courses; and among credit-earning and non-credit or experiential learning. The landscape of what constitutes credible, viable, accessible, and valued learning options has become vastly more complex. It is more complicated for students and for institutions to understand, to make sensible decisions about, and to act within.

Given institutions' inherent levels of self-interest, the natural desire for self-preservation, and the decades during which institutions focused on data and information about what occurred on the premises but not in other learning environments, it is simply too early to predict what the real impact of distance education will be on institutional research. What is not too early to predict is that there will be an impact.

Notes

1. NPEC was created in 1994, when Congress authorized the National Center for Education Statistics to create a cooperative with a mission "to identify and communicate ongoing and merging issues germane to postsecondary education and to promote the quality, comparability, and utility of postsecondary data and information that support policy development, implementation, and evaluation." NPEC comprises individuals representing all levels of postsecondary education, as well as statewide governing and coordinating agencies, federal government agencies, and national associations.

2. I am indebted to Nofflet Williams, former associate dean for distance learning at the University of Kentucky, for suggesting to me that distance education may well be the agent provocateur in the assessment arena, finally forcing traditionalists to take assessment seriously.

References

Adelman, C. "What Proportion of College Students Earn a Degree?" *AAHE Bulletin,* 1998, 51 (2), 7–9.

Armajani, B., Heydinger, R., and Hutchinson, P. *A Model for the Reinvented Higher Education System: State Policy and College Learning.* Denver: State Higher Education Executive Officers and Education Commission of the States, 1994.

Berge, Z. L., and Schrum, L. "Linking Strategic Planning with Program Implementation for Distance Education." *CAUSE/EFFECT,* 1998, 21 (3), 31–38.

Bolman, L. G., and Deal, T. E. *Reframing Organizations: Artistry, Choice, and Leadership.* San Francisco: Jossey-Bass, 1991.

Cartwright, G. P. "Technology Implications for Data Systems." *Change,* July–August 1998, pp. 48–50.

Couchman, J. "Becoming a Certified Oracle DBA." *Oracle Magazine,* November–December 1998, pp. 125–130.

Dolence, M. G. "Dawn of the Learning Age." Paper presented at the Thirty-Second Annual National Conference of the Council for Resource Development, Washington, D.C., Dec. 3, 1998.

Ewell, P. T. "Assessing Student Progress and Learning Gains." In U.S. Department of Education, National Center for Education Statistics. *Technology and Its Ramifications for Data Systems: Report of the Policy Panel on Technology.* Publication no. NCES 98-279. Washington, D.C.: National Postsecondary Education Cooperative, 1998.

Guernsey, L. "A New Career Track Combines Teaching and Academic Computing." *Chronicle of Higher Education,* Dec. 11, 1998, pp. A35–A37.

Institute for Higher Education Policy. "Distance Learning in Higher Education." *CHEA Chronicle,* 1999, 2(1), 1–8.

Jewett, F. "Benefits and Costs of Mediated Instruction Summary." [www.calstate.edu /special_projects/mediated_instr/summary.html]. Jan. 25, 1999.

Jones, D. "Managing Faculty Assets to Accommodate New Realities." *NCHEMS News,* Feb. 1999, pp. 2–5.

McLean, R. S. "Assessing Course Assignments Submitted as Web Pages." [www.oise .utoronto.ca/~rmclean]. Jan. 13, 1999.

Mingle, J. R., and Ruppert, S. S. *Technology Planning: State and System Issues.* Denver: Education Commission of the States, 1998.

Packer, A. H. "A Community Human Resource Network." Unpublished paper, Institute for Policy Studies, Johns Hopkins University, July 23, 1998.

Privateer, P. M. "Academic Technology and the Future of Higher Education: Strategic Paths Taken and Not Taken." *Journal of Higher Education,* 1999, *70* (1), 60–79.

Russell, A. B. "Advances in Statewide Higher Education Data Systems." Unpublished paper available through State Higher Education Executive Officers, Oct. 1995.

Russell, T. L. *The No Significant Difference Phenomenon.* Raleigh: Office of Instructional Telecommunications, North Carolina State University, 1999.

U.S. Department of Education, National Center for Education Statistics. *Technology and Its Ramifications for Data Systems: Report of the Policy Panel on Technology.* Publication no. NCES 98-279. Washington, D.C.: National Postsecondary Education Cooperative, 1998.

TRUDY BERS is senior director of research, curriculum, and planning at Oakton Community College in Des Plaines, Illinois. She has been chairperson of the National Postsecondary Education Cooperative and president of the Association of Institutional Research. She can be reached at tbers@oakton.edu.

5

Based on the central trends discussed in this volume, this chapter provides a detailed scenario of the future IR (or IRPT) office and discusses the challenges ahead.

The Future IR Office

Liz Sanders

Information technology is changing the face of institutional research. But this is not a new phenomenon. Once-new technologies such as mainframe and personal computers allowed institutional researchers to use software packages to analyze data and more easily edit research reports. What is striking today, however, is the rate of change driven by advances in information technology—in computers, networks, and telecommunications—and the sustained rate of change pervasive in higher education.

At a recent national conference on the nature of stresses on research and higher education, Duderstadt (1999) noted that administrators and faculty raised a number of critical issues, yet interestingly, the impact of information technology was not explicitly among them. These discussions made it clear, however, that the stresses mentioned, such as concerns about indirect costs and government reporting and accountability requirements, were only symptoms of the impact of more fundamental forces driving change, many of which related directly to emerging technologies.

The chapters in this volume explore the ways in which these emerging technologies, often in conjunction with other trends, have affected the IR office. The authors discuss emerging technology trends in the corporate sector that are relevant to higher education, the dual challenge of both open information access and pressures for accountability, how technology can be used to transform IR functions, and how IR has been affected by technology's imprint on learning and pedagogy. From these discussions, three general themes emerge: the role of information technology as a catalyst for change, the meaning of open access to information both inside and outside the institution, and the new information professional in general and, specifically, the new technology-savvy institutional researcher.

Information Technology as a Catalyst for Change

Throughout the volume, the authors discuss how advances in information technology continue to transform what we do and how we do it. New technologies call us to rethink how we deliver our products and services as they break down traditional barriers and create new opportunities for connecting with our customers, our students, and each other. As Chan notes in Chapter One, advances in high-speed communication, storage, and microprocessor technologies and the digitization of information have propelled this change. Multicampus, high-speed networks and the Internet and World Wide Web technologies have further accelerated this change by creating new ways to share information and relate to our colleagues and customers. This transformation has been extensive, from the most basic to the most complex tasks. For example, information technology has all of the following effects:

- It allows us to streamline our more basic tasks of data collection and storage using networks and databases.
- It makes compliance with reporting easier with on-line survey submissions and data collection software, allowing us greater flexibility in reviewing and updating data.
- It changes our relationship with our customers and constituents, allowing us to provide information, reports, and various data virtually on demand using various database and Internet or intranet technologies, and allows us to interact with our customers electronically.
- It changes our relationship with one another, creating opportunities for telecommuting, electronic collaboration, and new electronic partnerships both on and off campus.
- It urges us to promote the notion of the student-centered experience, through the development of new learning technologies centered around the student's individual learning needs and new information systems that empower the customer to conduct much of the business of education electronically.
- It changes how we define key variables for study by challenging us to explore interinstitutional definitions for things like the student transcript.
- It provides us with new research questions and new opportunities to integrate external information and experience into our work.
- It calls us to serve as information architects and planners in the strategic design and development of these information and knowledge structures.
- It challenges us to rethink our place in the institution.

These challenges are often augmented by our own institution's readiness for change. Implementing new technology solutions is difficult without an institutional culture that is ready to accept change or in the absence of sufficient resources, infrastructure, or incentives. This is particularly important because recent technological advances have introduced a perplexing paradox. Advances in information technology, including more powerful and user-friendlier software and networking, have pushed the capacities of technology down to users, decentralizing access to information, analysis, and reporting capabilities and empowering users. At the same time, however, strong and developed technology infrastructure and strategic information technology planning are crucial to the success of this decentralization. Chan notes in Chapter One that the successful implementation of all four corporate sector approaches, from knowledge management to electronic commerce, depends on a mature technology infrastructure. Without it, the implementation of new systems can be slow and costly. Similarly, one-third of the institutions in a recent study of distance learning (Lewis, Alexander, and Farris, 1997) cited limited technological infrastructure to support distance learning as a reason for not starting or expanding current program offerings. IR professionals can help guide their institutions through this assessment of readiness to help ensure that the implementation of technology solutions will be successful.

Pressures of Access and Accountability

The interconnectivity created by advances in technology is even more powerful when coupled with other critical challenges higher education must face. These include increasing demands for services coupled with rising costs, increased public ambivalence toward education funding, and increasing public demands for accountability and demonstrated value. In Chapter Two, Wells, Silk, and Torres discuss how the forces of accountability, coupled with technology advances that have led to open access to information, have affected the IR office.

The authors note that institutions, under pressure from various constituents to demonstrate outcomes and performance, turn to the IR office to gather, analyze, and disseminate information that can be used to demonstrate accountability. Policy pieces begin to supplement the more traditional IR functions of data collection and reporting. Recent advances in networking and telecommunications have augmented this pressure. With greater access to information, external agencies, legislators, and the media can now review institutional data that were at one time available only in aggregate reports. For example, through advances in electronic data submission and Web access to various raw data sources such as IPEDS, a state education policy committee can easily access and quickly download a large block of institutional enrollment and financial data for several consecutive years in order to draw policy implications to shape funding allocation.

Open access brings with it, however, the possibility of misinterpretation and misrepresentation. Information that is available electronically often includes documentation that must be thoroughly examined to unravel the complexities of the data. For example, IPEDS data documentation provides information about the differences in survey forms, survey methodology, and coding issues. This, however, gives the user only a partial understanding of the complexity of the data. The raw data and their documentation do not contain important contextual information that allows the user to understand the trends fully and interpret them. For example, dips in the numbers of new freshmen enrolled at a particular institution may reflect planned curriculum changes or unforeseen sluggish recruitment. IR offices are called on to review, reevaluate, and respond to these third-party interpretations of institutional data.

Of course, access also provides the institutional researcher with a variety of new resources with which to respond to these challenges. Easy access to external databases, benchmarking data from other institutions, and even streamlined internal data allow institutional researchers to understand the issues better and provide contextual intelligence for the decision maker. The U.S. Department of Education's Web site (www.ed.gov) provides access to a wide variety of information, including options to download raw data, statistical reports, regulations, or policy pieces or to query databases on-line. The *Chronicle of Higher Education's* Web site (chronicle.com/infotech) provides details about current information technology initiatives such as the Association of American Publishers' guide to on-line information about metadata. The researcher can also find information on statistics (for example, The Chance Database, designed to help students understand the use of probability and statistics, at www.geom.umn.edu/docs/snell/chance /welcome.html). Optimizing these external sources requires time and resources, however. For data sources, documentation and data integrity must be carefully researched, as the institutional researcher is not above misinterpretation or misrepresentation.

In Chapter Two, Wells, Silk, and Torres discuss how institutional researchers can play a significant role in designing, developing, and overseeing new open-access information systems in their emerging role as information architects. In this role, the new IR office can provide guidance and vision in the system and policy development. These may include the development of streamlined on-campus systems such as client-server and ERP systems, campus intranets, and networked databases. They may also include policies and practices for access and using off-campus information.

Joining with the information technology unit on campus, IR information architects can provide valuable input from the perspective of both information user and creator, as well as necessary oversight of information content and integrity. Information architects guide the discussions of institutional readiness and leveraging technology strategically in both the administrative and academic arenas.

The New Information Professional

Challenges to higher education also come from changing forces in society, demographic trends, and emerging social needs, which, when coupled with advances in instructional and information technologies, signal increased competition for a new market of information professionals (Blustain, Gold-stein, and Lozier, 1999; Council for Aid to Education, 1995). One example of this convergence is the changing relationship between employers and employees. Today lifetime employment is no longer an expectation. Often employees must continually retool and retrain to stay current in their field and thus marketable. Recent advances in networking and the Internet make education service delivery easier and more flexible and allow higher education to meet the education needs of the working professional. Together, the coupling of changes in society and technology creates a dynamic environment for higher education, opening new markets of working professionals who demand more flexible education services from higher education or other willing providers and redefining the knowledge, skills, and abilities of education information professionals, including institutional researchers.

New Market Opportunities. Advances in instructional technologies have changed the way higher education serves the needs of adult working professionals, one of higher education's most promising markets. These professionals have different educational expectations and needs than traditional-age undergraduates. They demand easy access to programs and services, convenient schedules for classes and program completion, customized curriculum, flexible delivery, and higher standards of technology (Blustain, Goldstein, and Lozier, 1999).

To meet these needs, distance learning offerings have exploded, as Bers notes in Chapter Four. She points out that forty states have adopted virtual university strategies and there are already over one million on-line learners (Dolence, 1998). Using technology that breaks down barriers of time and space, education service providers can now deliver educational products and services anywhere, anytime. Working professionals can take courses toward a degree or certificate at their desktops during the lunch hour or at home in the evening after their children have gone to bed.

Higher education is not alone in this market, however, and must now face a new kind of competition from for-profit enterprises. Katz (1999) notes that although institutions rarely frame their policies and practices in competitive terms, the emergence of technology-based education delivery systems and pressures on existing resources will change this. He notes, for example, that an independent for-profit corporation called the Home Education Network has acquired the right to distribute UCLA Extension's courses. In addition, the University of Phoenix, a subsidiary of the publicly traded Apollo Group, has demonstrated substantial revenues and provides educational services across a large part of the United States. Recently, Jones International University, which specializes in selling on-line courses, became the first Internet-only school to be accredited to grant college degrees (Gehl and Douglas, 1999).

To compete in this market, Bers notes that higher education institutions must think strategically about how to leverage distance learning programs most effectively as part of a comprehensive package of educational services and how to position themselves in this new landscape of education service providers. Institutional researchers can play a crucial role in helping their institutions shape these policies and prepare for the impact of distance education growth and competition.

The dramatic rise in distance learning offerings also affects the traditional functions of the IR office. IR offices will need to rethink the meaning of such basic parameters as student population, faculty workload, and course credit hour. Understanding educational outcomes will become more complicated and require greater collaboration across institutions, when students may during one semester take courses from more than one institution, some in a traditional classroom and some via electronic instruction. These changes will require the institutional researcher to work proactively and collaboratively with decision makers and colleagues to sort out the impact of distance education.

The New Information Professional. Nowhere is this notion of continuous professional retooling more critical than in the area of information technology. Advances in technology have had a significant impact on education knowledge professionals. For example, at my institution, the public relations office now devotes a sizable portion of its time to publishing materials electronically, developing and policing the institution's Web site, and communicating electronically with external constituents. To do this, staff may be required to develop a variety of new technical skills in networking, software, hardware installation, and programming. A staff writer may spend more time focusing on Web publishing than producing paper materials and must learn networking skills and how to use HTML to convert print documents, organize material on the Web, and provide navigational tools for readers. In addition, our university library has embraced a variety of new technologies to assist students, faculty, and staff with research and learning. Technologies that allow electronic access to off-campus materials enable the library to expand its virtual holdings, and digital technologies have allowed the library to expand user access to a variety of rare or unique collections.

These new hybrid information professionals must be knowledgeable not only in their fields but also in harnessing the latest high-tech tools once reserved for the computer programmer. They often play a critical role in championing the design, development, and use of new information technologies, systems, and networks. As Chan notes in Chapter One, essentially everyone will become a technology user.

The new technology-savvy institutional researcher is also part of this group of hybrid, high-tech information professionals. In their case studies, Schaefer and Massa in Chapter Three provide insight into the challenges the new technology-wise IR professional must face. They describe how, by embracing information technology solutions, IR professionals have been required to develop new skills in database development and administration, networking, programming, and information systems. As noted by these authors, the expectations for information technology are high, but the reality is often, at least initially, slow, complex, and costly. Campus users who are enamored of high-tech solutions or the capacities of technology may not see these hidden costs, however, and instead focus on the "point and click" nature of the information or report. This perspective can be problematic for the IR office as it seeks to garner additional resources for new high-tech projects, new hybrid staff, or professional development and training. Using technology will require relearning, retooling, and a redistribution of resources.

A Vision of Technology's Transformations

These themes recur throughout the volume—technology is changing how we learn, work, and share our information. The President's Information Technology Advisory Committee (1998), in its interim report on future directions for federal support of research and development in high performance computing, communications, information technology, and the next-generation Internet, highlighted several ways in which information technology will transform our lives. Three critical visions are relevant to this volume:

- The vision of the transformation of how we learn: "Any individual can participate in on-line education programs regardless of geographic location, age, physical limitations, or personal schedule. Everyone can access repositories of educational materials, easily recalling past lessons, updating skills, or selecting from among different teaching methods in order to discover the most effective style for that individual. Educational programs can be customized to each individual's needs, so that our information revolution reaches everyone and no one gets left behind" (p. 9).
- The vision of the transformation of how we work: "The workplace is no longer confined to a specific geographic location, as workers can easily access their tasks and colleagues from alternate locations or while en route. Workers have access to jobs without regard to physical proximity to major metropolitan areas. They can choose where they live based on nearness to family or lifestyle preference rather than job market opportunities. A highly flexible workplace is able to accommodate each individual's needs, from working parents to workers with disabilities" (p. 10).
- The vision of the transformation of the way we deal with information: "An individual can access, query, or print any book, magazine, newspaper, video, data item, or reference document in any language by simply clicking the mouse, touching the computer screen, talking to the computer, or blinking an eye. Individuals can easily select among modes of presentation: data, text, images, or audio. Information can be referenced and derivations can be incorporated in networks and software-enabled tools" (p. 9).

These visions of technology's impact provide a framework for the new IR office. This office will draw heavily from the traditions of the profession,

new advances in information and instructional technologies, and the changing nature of decision making in higher education. Several institutional
researchers, including those in this volume, have discussed how the role of
the IR office should be broadened for the next century (Matier, Sidle, and
Hurst, 1995). In addition to handling its traditional functions of the collection, analysis, and dissemination of information to support decision making, the IR office should also serve as information architect and change
agent. The role of IR is as important as ever because decision makers in this
changing higher education environment require a comprehensive understanding of the institution and solid strategic planning skills to guide its
future. From these chapters, we have seen that IR can provide

- Valuable knowledge about the institution and its place in the education
  market
- Valuable input that can guide institutional change and support strategic
  planning and management of scarce resources
- Expertise in understanding the impact of instructional technology
  through student assessment, program evaluation, and studies to determine market feasibility and use of resources
- Guidance and expertise as information architects of tomorrow's information systems

The Emerging Institutional Research
and Technology Office

Let me take you now to an IR office in the not-too-distant future. Perhaps
the reader already works in such an institutional research, planning, and
information technology office.

Midwest University. At Midwest University (MU), a for-profit institution with campuses in ten midwestern cities, the undergraduate learning
experience is based on a blending of on-line and in-class learning. The
undergraduate residential college environment provides a unique opportunity to experience what it means to "live and learn." Students in the Chicago
performing arts living center communicate regularly with students in the
Minneapolis performing arts living center via videoconference study groups
and electronic course chat rooms. Undergraduates attend classes taught
down the hall or across the country.

The graduate programs also blend instructional technology and traditional classroom learning. The university provides a variety of degree and
certification programs for traditional full-time graduate students and part-
time employed students wishing to upgrade their skills. For example, the
graduate business program competes internationally for students who take
only on-line courses at their work computer or via their interactive television in the privacy of their own homes. The evening courses in finance are
taught by a Fortune 500 financial analyst from his desk in New York City.

The College of Sciences uses Web technology to provide actual laboratory experiences for students who take off-site courses.

At all levels, on-campus courses are taught in "smart classrooms" that allow faculty to "bring in" researchers from other institutions or experiments in other labs during class, as well as static resources from the Internet. For example, in the College of Social Sciences, students in the Political Science Department use smart classrooms to sit in the gallery of a European Community Parliament discussion or to visit the dig site of a faculty member in Africa to learn about the latest archaeological findings.

Students can register, complete and monitor financial aid, check grades, buy books, and choose housing electronically. In addition, a consortium of institutions also provides comprehensive course catalogues and class schedules on-line to facilitate cross-registration. Student Services maintains a twenty-four-hour-a-day, seven-day-a-week hotline for student calls and also provides information on the Web regarding policies, frequently asked questions, and emergency procedures.

IRPT Office. Six professional staff located in three different cities staff the central Institutional Research, Planning, and Technology (IRPT) office. Two work part time at MU and are based at a large education research consulting firm. The professional staff are experienced in both current research techniques and technologies; professional development and training opportunities are provided to the staff in both areas. Each location also has support staff and computer information systems professionals.

The IRPT director reports to the vice president for planning, to whom also report the director for academic planning and the director for information technology. Prior to this, the Information Technology unit, which managed technology operations, was under the vice president for business operations, and the distance learning unit, which coordinated instructional technology for the institution, was separately located in the graduate school.

This organizational structure was the outgrowth of a planning retreat several years ago in which institutional leaders determined that the efforts to advance instructional technologies and on-line course offerings were not fully integrated into academic curriculum planning. Leaders felt that information technology planning had been marginalized. For example, the graduate school focused its distance learning resources on providing programs to the regional, part-time student market. This had been a large revenue generator for MU for several years, and demand was projected to continue to be strong. For this reason, the Math Department developed on-line courses for part-time graduate students only and did not integrate them into program planning for full-time, research-based graduate students and undergraduates. At this time, the separate MU campuses were not fully interconnected, and little effort was being made to move in that direction.

At the retreat, leaders identified two other critical markets for instructional technology efforts. MU felt that it could successfully compete for the national and international working professional market, and by focusing efforts to interconnect its campuses fully, it could also compete for a larger share of the undergraduate market by integrating technology into residential living and other on-campus programs. MU selected information technology as the cornerstone of its new strategic plan.

One outcome of the retreat was to create the office of the vice president for planning, which would provide leadership in infusing visionary planning in information technology into academic and administrative areas. The university leadership repositioned the directors of information technology and academic planning together under this umbrella. The IR office was added to this group and expanded to include a recognized focus on technology and renamed the IRPT office. In this structure, information technology in both the academic and administrative areas was coordinated from this office, and a closer linkage between academic planning and information technology was developed.

This restructuring radically changed the nature of the IR office. Once focused on conducting social science research and planning and data functions and staffed by education and social science research Ph.D. professionals, the office underwent a radical period of retraining that resulted in high staff turnover, difficult rehiring, and low morale. Since this restructuring, however, the staffing has been more stable. To maximize the benefits of new technologies, staff are given options for flextime, work-at-home time, and professional development training. Because of the unique skill sets and marketability of these researcher-technology experts, compensation packages are now competitive with the private sector.

An additional reason for this morale boost was the vice president's efforts to build a collaborative work climate. All staff under the VP work closely together in cross-functional teams on various projects. This approach integrates the unique skills of each unit and has been successful in providing solutions that are more strongly grounded in MU's strategic plan. For example, recently the unit collaborated to update the MU Information Technology Strategic Plan.

The unit continues to struggle, however, with several internal issues related to this new role. For example, planning and setting priorities have become more complicated due to the expanding number and types of project stakeholders. This expansion has also affected the areas of staff development and performance review. The director has developed three strategies that have been moderately successful to address these concerns. First, the director relies on guidance from the vice president and the institution's strategic plan when planning the office agenda. Recently this has led to several technical projects' taking priority over more traditional research projects and caused some frustration among the staff. In addition, the VP's entire unit has created a strategic plan and project agenda that is reviewed and approved annually by the president's cabinet and tied closely to the strategic plan. Second, the director developed a client evaluation tool to be used at the completion of all projects, internal or external, that provides structured individual feedback for the staff development and review process. Third, staff keep track of time spent on each project. The director uses this information to monitor project costs and project load to ensure that external projects do not dominate the agenda. Let us look at a few of IRPT's current projects.

Federal and State Mandatory Reporting. All required information reporting is done on-line. As a function of the institution's networking, a staff member from the Kansas City office works with a researcher from St. Louis to complete the IPEDS as if she were in the office next door. All workstations (those in the office and at home, where many of the staff work part time) are equipped with video cameras and daily teleconferencing is routine.

MU Information Infrastructure. The IRPT director is currently staffing a committee to review and recommend the next legacy system for all transactional nonrelational central systems. These systems have a series of Web interfaces developed by the IT division that allow greater user functionality and have served to delay systems replacement to funnel IT resources to other strategic priorities, including teleconferencing projects, the laptop program for students, and data warehousing projects. One of these strategic priorities, the MU intranet, facilitates sharing a wide variety of institutional resources. The intranet was built by a collaborative team of IRPT and IT staff, which provides both technical and content supervision on an ongoing basis.

In addition, the IRPT director chaired an institutional committee to develop MU's Institutional Information Warehouse (IIW). The programming is maintained by a workgroup of IRPT and IT staff. The IIW provides a data warehouse of information from across all institutional functions that can be accessed by all MU staff. The IRPT office has used the IIW, as well as the Department of Education Knowledge Network, to develop a series of point-and-click icons to generate special reports that are delivered on-line in spreadsheet and graphical formats to users over the intranet. Currently, the team is developing a voice-prompt interface that allows users to query the IIW more easily.

During the development of the IIW, IRPT closely examined the current data policies and procedures related to the transactional systems and several of the school's shadow systems. After identifying several gaps in data integrity and maintenance, and in light of current technologies that expand access to information dramatically, IRPT formed a committee to monitor data access, control, and integrity.

MU's Factbook. When the IIW is updated annually, a series of report generators designed by IRPT create the MU factbook. A small number of factbooks are still printed on paper, as requested by several of the academic units heads, and the document is available on the intranet. Users can query the data and produce text or graphical reports.

Peer School Collaboration Warehouse and Standard Survey. Through a reasonably smooth collaboration with regional, national, and international peer institutions, IRPT and other IR offices have developed a common data set warehouse and report generator. For all collaborating institutions, this warehouse provides information for ad hoc information requests. The warehouse also automatically generates an updated standard survey for each college and delivers these electronically to guidebook publishers. The standard survey is accessible on the intranet.

MU Study of Student Attendance Patterns. As a result of pressures from funding agencies following an unflattering state-level report on undergraduate attendance patterns and completion rates, the institution chose to reexamine its student attendance patterns. After an initial review of the student records data and a multi-institution study of cross-enrollments, IRPT persuaded the institution to forge an agreement with a large consortium of peer institutions to develop a student credit bank, replacing outdated articulation agreements and streamlining student tracking. Once these difficult and time-consuming negotiations have been completed, a study of student attendance patterns will be conducted jointly by IR staff representing this consortium. Groupware and teleconferencing technology will allow the staff to work together on this project electronically.

Student Satisfaction Survey. Student satisfaction survey data collection is done on-line, using a Web interface and database collection process developed and maintained by the IRPT office. Both students and parents are contacted electronically for information; parents can complete their portions of the survey at home via their interactive television or at work, and parents often work together with their children to provide feedback to the institution. The report is available for students and parents on the Web, and historical data are housed in a database that is available on the MU intranet for internal ad hoc reporting.

A large portion of the recent student survey assessed student satisfaction with the availability of personal one-on-one contact with their faculty and advisers. The Advancement Office is concerned that students who take courses only on-line are not developing a strong connection with the institution. They feel that there is more the institution can do but desire solid information on which to base an action plan. The IRPT office has been contracted to study the factors that produce the kind of student commitment to the university that leads to persistence and will soon complete the development of a set of indicators that will better reflect high-tech student, faculty, and adviser interactions.

Strategic Planning. The IRPT office has just completed preparations for the annual strategic planning conference, opening with a series of virtual sessions with national education and peer school planners at other locations and continuing with live sessions for planners from all campuses. After an extensive report on MU's market position, drawn from electronic access to a variety of sources of external scanning information, MU seeks to explore new niche programs emphasizing MU's unique strengths, as well as collaborative joint programs with peers, and to identify resulting competition. Hardware and software compatibility issues slowed the conference planning and required additional resources for upgrades, testing, and technical support.

Student Outcomes Assessment. Another facet of the conference will be to plan for the upcoming accreditation visit and review progress with the E-Folio project. MU's regional accreditation board coordinated efforts several years ago to develop an electronic student portfolio software with the assistance of faculty, institutional researchers, and information technology professionals from various schools, including MU. This was done in response to faculty resistance to assessment efforts reported at many institutions and based in part on issues of workload. The accreditation board determined that streamlining data management would improve faculty acceptance of assessment.

The software contains a standard portfolio that can be customized by each school or department for discipline-specific requirements and standard reporting tools. At MU, each student receives the portfolio software during the application process and submits samples of high school work for review. The student continues to maintain the portfolio through graduation. The Career Transitions Office houses the student portfolio material and provides scanning equipment and other hardware and software for student use.

Working closely with the faculty, a team of IRPT and IT staff customized the on-line portfolio evaluation tool for managing and reviewing student portfolios to meet the specific needs of MU and the participating departments and developed a series of portfolio policies covering access and evaluation procedures. This process was slow and often difficult. Faculty participation has been slow to develop, and departments have been slow to agree on customization issues. Additional time was also needed to consult with the general counsel about the legal issues related to accessing student information in general and via the Internet specifically. Because internal and external access to information has expanded dramatically, IRPT routinely seeks the advice of the general counsel when developing systems or data projects that create or change data access relationships.

Instead of developing a separate assessment warehouse, the team developed a virtual database by programming a series of point-and-click reports that link the portfolio assessment information to the data warehouse and the transactional database. Faculty participating on the assessment committee can easily review documents on the Intranet and use report and assessment tools to evaluate student progress.

In addition, to assist the Career Transitions Office, the team developed a series of tools for employers, once a student has requested that the portfolio be viewable to external audiences. These include a standard electronic transcript, résumé, letters of recommendation, and static and dynamic work samples. One student's portfolio contains a live video feed to his student teaching classroom during his teaching times.

Staff Survey. Three years ago, the president's cabinet was concerned about the level of turnover at the middle administration level. After a survey of staff morale, marketability, and career development, conducted by IRPT, the cabinet made significant changes in the culture of work at MU. This year, a follow-up survey will be conducted to assess the impact of the new telecommuting policy and the professional development policy.

Telecommuting policy. Staff are permitted to take annual appointments in sister offices at other sites (now considered by MU as a temporary company transfer). A staff member has the option of telecommuting to the new location and is provided with a standard-model PC for home use, complete with videoconferencing capability. Staff are also permitted telecommuting options to their home institutions. All staff can also participate in private office chat rooms to facilitate staff communication across units at different locations.

Since continuity of student contact is considered important at MU, staff with student contact are on call for students, who can e-mail, videoconference, or telephone staff members as needed. For staff with a great deal of student contact who request a temporary company transfer, special arrangements are made to accommodate student needs and maintain this continuity.

Professional development policy. After a two-year employment period, staff may apply for a semesterlong development sabbatical. During this time, staff may attend MU or another peer institution or may propose professional development activities to be completed during this time. After this initial leave, employees are eligible to apply for similar leaves every five years. A large proportion of the sabbaticals that were granted during the first year were for staff requesting retraining in new hardware, software, and networking technologies.

Institutional Policies and Procedures. All institutional business is done electronically, and all faculty, students, and staff are issued laptops with docking ports, unless special capacities for graphics, processing, or storage are required. Computer upgrades are managed centrally, while software is managed locally. Staff conduct all institutional business on the intranet (for example, purchase orders, payroll authorizations, and check disbursement vouchers).

The Higher Education Services Extranet allows staff to conduct all business with outsourced services (for example, marketing, publications, food services, bookstore) and other vendors (for example, office supplies, computer software services, facilities maintenance) electronically. Purchasing, billing, scheduling, and delivery are all handled on-line.

The Future. Is this your office of the future? For many IR offices, parts of these activities are already in place. For example, my office is routinely involved in database projects and employs part-time computer science students knowledgeable in programming languages to develop interfaces with networked databases. We use this technology to develop internal tracking mechanisms such as a procedures database and an information request database and to collect data during survey research. We routinely distribute office reports via e-mail, not campus mail, with postings available on our Web site. For staff, technical training is included as part of the annual professional development budget, through a redistribution of resources, not additional funds.

However, for many offices, these technology-savvy functions and roles are still evolving, as a recent survey of IR technology utilization indicated (Noble, Borden, and Massa, 1999). About half of the institutional researchers who participated in this survey said they *never* developed or maintained data warehouses and data marts (46 percent), used Web site developer software (51 percent), or used desktop publishing software (58 percent). Almost three in four IR staff (71 percent) said they had never used programming or scripting languages. IR professionals expect, however, that use of a variety of technologies, including using the Web to access information, will increase over the next two years.

Challenges for Today's IR Office

Today, IR offices face a variety of challenges due to recent advances in technology. The chapters in this volume have examined these challenges, from corporate sector technology trends that can be adapted to the needs of education to the impact of instructional technology development on IR functions. Three themes have emerged. First, technology is an agent for change in higher education. It is changing our work and our profession. Second, the combined pressures of accountability and open access information systems have challenged many IR offices to assume new roles as policy analyst, college advocate, and information architect. Three important skills in this new IR toolbox are developing information systems, providing contextual grounding for information users in decentralized information systems, and responding to external interpretations of institutional information. Third, advances in instructional technologies have changed the way institutions interface with the adult working professional. Distance education challenges the IR office to rethink the basics, such as the meaning of student credit hours, and to reconceptualize institutions as independent, autonomous entities. Technology has also created hybrid information professionals, adept in both their professional content areas and in various technologies, who play a critical role in higher education. This hybrid professional is a role model for the new technology-savvy institutional researcher.

Advances in technology will continue to transform our profession—how we learn, work, and share information. Based on the vision of tomorrow presented in this volume, there are several opportunities and challenges related to information flow, research, and information technology systems development for today's IR office:

• IR must embrace technology as a means of streamlining the flow of information and research functions and of empowering information users. It must provide quicker, easier access to data and information with tools to enable users to conduct ad hoc queries on demand. With this comes the challenge of educating the user in using new software, hardware, and information systems and in the realities of providing these high-tech solutions. Streamlining internal information and creating open access systems challenges IR to take an active role as college advocate in providing the user, on or off campus, with ample context and background information in order to minimize the possibility of data misuse. As a college advocate, the institutional researcher must also try to allocate sufficient time in the research agenda to respond to misrepresented information. The researcher may need to conduct additional analyses or write special reports to clarify misinterpretations.

• IR must strive to provide a contextual grounding in research and planning materials to provide the user with richer and more useful support for decision making. We must develop tools that allow for greater access to external information to provide better decision support and use this access to foster a broad focus in research by, for example, including benchmarking information in standard reports when available. The cost of these tools, both financial and staffing, and the contextual issues associated with these external data should be carefully evaluated.

• IR must provide strategic guidance in developing the institution's information technology systems. As an information architect, the IR professional brings a unique insight into the needs of the information user and provider and can provide needed data integrity and content oversight. This role also allows the IR professional to function as an advocate for thoughtfully implementing technological solutions and technology-based redesigned processes.

As part of this, the IR office should create an IR strategic plan and comprehensively evaluate office resources needed to implement technology-based solutions in order to allocate staff and financial resources adequately. Different agendas require different resources, support, on-campus collaborations, and reporting lines. The challenge is to develop a balanced agenda of research and information technology that can be adequately staffed and supported, often with few additional resources.

• IR must ask "Should we?" rather than "Can we?" Critically evaluate the costs and benefits of technology solutions. Just because the technology is available to change a low-tech process into a high-tech process, this does not mean the high-tech process is more effective or efficient. Carefully evaluate the additional costs of technology solutions outside of the obvious hardware and software costs, such as training, technical support, and staff skills retooling, and be aware of how these solutions will affect the organizational culture. This requires an assessment of the institution's readiness to undergo these changes. The right institutional climate and technology infrastructure are the keys to project success.

• IR must proactively engage in activities that seek to understand the impacts of information and instructional technologies on the user. Such activities will necessitate redefinition of traditional institutional concepts and processes and may require IR to take the lead in developing collaborative work groups inside and outside the institution to solve problems.

• The institution must provide the necessary professional development for retraining and retooling staff in critical skills, knowledge, and abilities. The new hybrid IR professional will be highly marketable and will require training and education incentives in both research content areas and technologies.

• Everyone should anticipate change as a perpetual state of affairs— change can be managed.

References

Blustain, H., Goldstein, P., and Lozier, G. "Assessing the New Competitive Landscape." In R. Katz (ed.), *Dancing with the Devil: Information Technology and the New Competition in Higher Education*. San Francisco: Jossey-Bass, 1999.

Council for Aid to Education. *Breaking the Social Contract: The Fiscal Crisis in Higher Education*. New York: Council for Aid to Education, 1995.

Dolence, M. G. "Dawn of the Learning Age." Paper presented at the Thirty-Second Annual National Conference of the Council for Resource Development, Washington, D.C., Dec. 3, 1998.

Duderstadt, J. "Can Colleges and Universities Survive in the Information Age?" In R. Katz (ed.), *Dancing with the Devil: Information Technology and the New Competition in Higher Education*. San Francisco: Jossey-Bass, 1999.

Gehl, J., and Douglas, S. "Online University Accredited to Grant Degrees." *Edupage Electronic Newsletter* [http://educause.unc.edu], Mar. 9, 1999.

Katz, R. "Competitive Strategies for Higher Education in the Information Age." In R. Katz (ed.), *Dancing with the Devil: Information Technology and the New Competition in Higher Education*. San Francisco: Jossey-Bass, 1999.

Lewis, L., Alexander, D., and Farris, E. *Distance Education in Higher Education Institutions*. Publication no. NCES 97-062. Washington, D.C.: U.S. Department of Education, National Center for Education Statistics, 1997.

Matier, W. M., Sidle, C. C., and Hurst, P. J. "Institutional Researchers' Roles in the Twenty-First Century." In T. R. Sanford (ed.), *Preparing for the Information Needs of the Twenty-First Century*. New Directions in Institutional Research, no. 85. San Francisco: Jossey Bass, 1995.

Noble, J., Borden, V., and Massa, T. "Technology Utilization." *AIR Electronic Newsletter*, Apr. 13, 1999.

President's Information Technology Advisory Committee. *Interim Report to the President*. Arlington, Va.: National Coordination Office for Computing, Information and Communications, 1998.

LIZ SANDERS is founder and director of the Office of Information and Institutional Research at Illinois Institute of Technology, Chicago, and can be reached at liz.sanders@iit.edu or on the Web at oiir.iit.edu.

INDEX

Knowledge repositories, 5
Knowledge structure, 5, 6
Knowledge transfer channels, 5

Laanan, F. S., 26, 39
Learner-centered data, 63
Learning, vision of transformation of, 85–86
Legacy systems: enterprise resource planning packages for, 8, 16; intranets for, 15–16, 17
Lenth, C. S., 25, 38
Lewis, L., 81, 95
Librarians, knowledge management and, 6, 7
LineSS, 16
Lohmann, D., 33, 38
Lotus Notes, 4, 19
Lozier, G., 83, 95

Maclag, L. S., 16, 20
Mainframe systems, 24–25
Marketing: data warehouses and, 13; institutional research role in, 32, 83–84, 87–88
Massa, T., 2, 25, 41, 60, 84–85, 93, 95
Massachusetts Institute of Technology (MIT), 16
Matier, W. M., 86, 95
McLean, R. S., 71, 78
Metadata, guide to, 82
Microprocessors, 3
Microsoft Access, 44, 45, 51
Microsoft certification program, 63
Microsoft Expedia, 15
Microsoft SQL server, 14
"Midwest University (MU)" Institutional Research, Planning, and Technology (IRPT) office, 86–93
Mingle, J. R., 73, 78
Multidimensional on-line analytical processing (MOLAP) systems, 13, 15
Multiple enrollment, 67, 68, 70, 74–75

National Association of Private Industry Councils, 29, 39
National Center for Higher Education Management Systems (NCHEMS), 65
National Postsecondary Education Cooperative (NPEC), 63–64, 76, 77n.1
National Student Loan Clearinghouse, 26

Nelson, K. R., 11, 20
No Significant Difference Phenomenon, The, 72
Noble, J., 93, 95
Nontraditional education: distance learning and, 61–64; impact of, on educational organizations, 62–64. See also Distance learning and education
Nonvolatility of data warehouses, 12
Normalization of database, 51
North Central Association of Colleges and Schools (NCA), 28, 44, 48
Novell certification program, 63
NTServer 4.0, 44

Oblinger, D. G., 3, 20
On-demand learning, knowledge networks for, 7
On-line analytic processing (OLAP) tools, 13, 15
Open database connectivity (ODBC), 45
Oracle, 8
Oracle Certified Database Administrator test, 62–63
Organizational structure, enterprise resource planning and, 8, 9
Organizations, knowledge management and, 5
Osborne, D., 23, 39
Outcomes measures, in new instructional delivery models, 64, 69–70, 91
Owens Corning, 8, 9
Ownership of data, 46

Packer, A. H., 68, 78
Pedagogy, knowledge networks for, 7
Peer school collaboration, 89–90
Pennsylvania State University Executive Information System, 14, 20
PeopleSoft, 8, 11
Performance-based funding, 27–29
Policies and procedures, Web publishing of, 55, 92
Porter, J. D., 13, 20
Portfolio assessment software, 91
President's Information Technology Advisory Committee, 85, 95
Privateer, P. M., 72, 74, 78
Process change: for enterprise resource planning, 8; for information technology approaches, compared, 19; for knowledge management, 6

Wild cards, 34–37
Willamette University (WU), Institutional Research and Planning Support (IRAPS), 49–57; cycles in, 49–50; database technology in, 50–53; new roles of, 56–58; overview of, 49; Web reports of, 55–57; Web technology in, 53, 55–57
Wolfe, R. J., 17, 20
Work, vision of transformation of, 85
Workforce Investment Act (WIA), 29
Works in progress, 70–71

Back Issue/Subscription Order Form

Copy or detach and send to:
Jossey-Bass Inc., Publishers, 350 Sansome Street, San Francisco CA 94104-1342

Call or fax toll free!
Phone 888-378-2537 6AM-5PM PST; Fax 800-605-2665

Back issues   Please send me the following issues at $23 each:
(Important: please include series initials and issue number, such as IR90)

1. IR _____

_____

_____

$ _____ Total for single issues

$ _____ Shipping charges (for single issues **only;** subscriptions are exempt
from shipping charges): Up to $30, add $5^{50} • $30^{01}–$50, add $6^{50}
$50^{01}–$75, add $7^{50} • $75^{01}–$100, add $9 • $100^{01}–$150, add $10
Over $150, call for shipping charge

Subscriptions   Please ❑ start   ❑ renew my subscription to *New Directions
for Institutional Research* for the year ____ at the following rate:

❑ Individual $56   ❑ Institutional $99
NOTE: Subscriptions are quarterly, and are for the calendar year only.
Subscriptions begin with the spring issue of the year indicated above.
For shipping outside the U.S., please add $25.

$ _____ Total single issues and subscriptions (CA, IN, NJ, NY and DC
residents, add sales tax for single issues. NY and DC residents must
include shipping charges when calculating sales tax. NY and Canadian
residents only, add sales tax for subscriptions.)

❑ Payment enclosed (U.S. check or money order only)

❑ VISA, MC, AmEx, Discover Card #_____ Exp. date_____

Signature _____ Day phone _____

❑ Bill me (U.S. institutional orders only. Purchase order required.)

Purchase order #_____

Name _____

Address _____

_____

_____

Phone_____ E-mail _____

For more information about Jossey-Bass Publishers, visit our Web site at:
www.josseybass.com   **PRIORITY CODE = ND1**

OTHER TITLES AVAILABLE IN THE NEW DIRECTIONS
FOR INSTITUTIONAL RESEARCH SERIES
J. Fredericks Volkwein, Editor-in-Chief

6578 012